Contents

KT-469-836

Geography words

Naming and describing

1 Word book

Give each child a book where he or she writes down and illustrates different geography words. This will help to extend the children's vocabulary and also help them with their spellings.

2 Geography dictionary

Differentiate for more able children by making a class or group dictionary with topic words and their definitions that children have found from dictionaries. Use small pictures to illustrate it.

Focus

- Talking about surroundings
- Using directional vocabulary
- Describing geographical features

3 Direction picture

Make up a display to illustrate directional words such as 'over', 'under', 'in front of' and 'behind'. Start by fixing strips of bright paper on to a wallboard. Then add each word in its correct position. Use these words as commands in PE.

4 Labels

Around a photograph or picture, place labels giving the words needed in a piece of work. Cover with plastic film so the children can match features to labels with Chinagraph pencil arrows.

A world of ideas

Activities and inspiration for primary geography

Stephen Scoffham and Sue Thomas

Stanley Thornes (Publishers) Ltd

1

Introduction

Geography is a varied subject that brings together many different parts of the school curriculum. It teaches children how to interpret their surroundings and understand the contemporary world. It also involves finding out about places overseas and learning a range of interpretive skills. This book illustrates different ways of teaching geography to children aged five to nine. Links with stories, music, modelling, artwork and Information Technology have been included whenever appropriate. The 'word banks', 'focus boxes' and 'teaching plans' highlight the main geographical ideas. We hope that the activities presented here will help teachers and students to introduce and develop geographical learning in an exciting way.

Acknowledgements

The work shown in this book was created in the following schools: • Amherst County Junior, Sevenoaks • Blean County Primary, Canterbury • Byron County Primary, Gillingham • East Peckham County Primary, Tonbridge • Frittenden CE Primary, Frittenden • Hythe County Infants, Hythe • Joy Lane County Infants, Whitstable • St. Peter's Methodist Primary, Canterbury • Sandling County Primary, Maidstone • Swalecliffe County Primary, Whitstable • Whitfield County Primary, Dover • Wrotham Road County Primary, Gravesend. We would like to thank all the children and staff involved.

Many people provided us with help but we would particularly like to thank the following:
Kathy Alcock, Jonathan Barnes, Janet Chapman, Terry Jewson, Sally Jones, Eleanor Watts, Tanya Whistance and students at Canterbury Christ Church College. Also Debbie Bartlett (Kent Property Services, Landscape), Linda Chimiczewski (Kent County Supplies), John Marshall and Mark Roberts (Canterbury Christ Church College AVA Dept) and Marion Walter (World Education Development Movement, East Kent).

The Sun Has Got His Hat On (page 11) Words and music by Ralph Butler and Noel Gay © 1932 Wests Ltd., 127 Charing Cross Road, London WC2H OEA / Richard Armitage Ltd., 8-9 Frith Street, London W1V 5TZ. Reproduced by permission. All rights reserved.
The Happy Wanderer (page 50) Words and music by F. W. Möller © Bosworth and Co. Ltd., 14/18 Heddon Street, Regent Street, London W1R 8DP. Reproduced by permission. All rights reserved.

Text © Stephen Scoffham and Sue Thomas 1997
Original line illustrations by Aetos Ltd. 1997 ©
Original photographs by Stephen Scoffham 1997 ©

The right of Stephen Scoffham and Sue Thomas to be identified as authors of this work has been asserted by them in accordance with the Copyright, Designs and Patents Act 1988.

All rights reserved. No part of this publication may be reproduced or transmitted in any form or by any means, electronic or mechanical, including photocopy, recording or any information storage and retrieval system, without permission in writing from the publisher or under licence from the Copyright Licensing Agency Limited. Further details of such licences (for reprographic reproduction) may be obtained from the Copyright Licensing Agency Limited, 90 Tottenham Court Road, London W1P 9HE.

First published in 1997 by:
Stanley Thornes (Publishers) Ltd
Ellenborough House
Wellington Street
CHELTENHAM GL50 1YW
England

97 98 99 00 01 / 10 9 8 7 6 5 4 3 2 1

A catalogue record for this book is available from the British Library
ISBN 0-7487-2477-X

Edited by Annie Scothern
Typeset by Aetos Ltd. Tadwick, Bath.
Printed in Hong Kong and bound in China by Dah Hua Printing Co.

5 Guessing game

Whisper one of the words you are using in a topic to a child or write it on a card. He or she must draw or describe the feature for the others to guess. The child who guesses correctly then has a turn to describe another feature.

6 Flow line

Long pictures that show the stages involved in making things can be fixed across the classroom wall like a timeline. Hang labels and drawings from the picture to make a mobile.

7 Class story

Children tell a story around the class, with each child adding a sentence or a phrase. Suitable themes include: a shipwreck, lost in the jungle and a world journey. Ask the children to make drawings to go with the different stages in the story. They could also represent it musically as a sound sequence.

8 Images of our town

Children brainstorm images of their town, listing all the things that contribute to its character. Use the words for a collage of four or more labelled pictures. Older children could design a town sign or a tourist logo from the images.

Weather

Weather conditions

1 Weather symbols

Get the children to devise symbols for rain, sun, wind, snow and other types of weather. Compare their designs with the standard symbols used in newspapers. You could watch a TV weather forecast to see how it is presented.

2 UK weather

This large outline weather map has small pieces of Velcro fixed to various areas. The children can move the symbols around to create a real or imaginary forecast. Their knowledge of the UK map will develop at the same time.

Focus

- Types of weather
- Observing and recording weather
- Effects of weather on people
- Weather in other places

Word bank

blizzard
fog
forecast
gale
ice
rainbow
shower
snow
storm
symbol
thunder

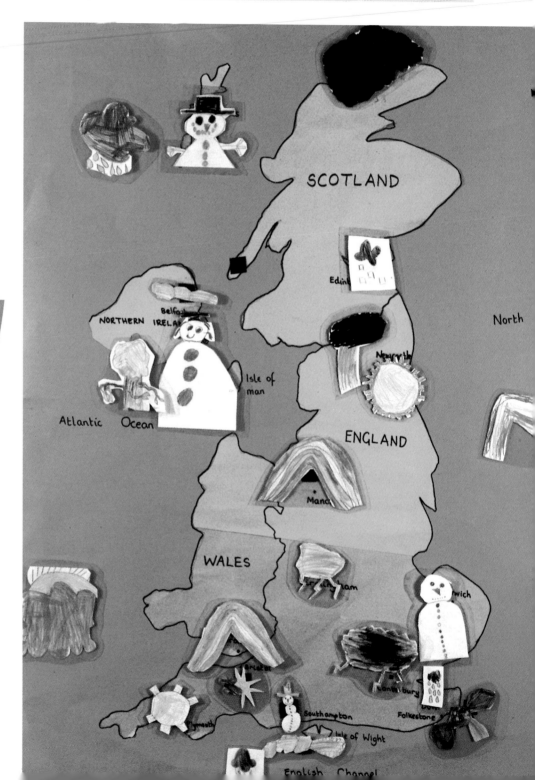

6 Weather Pelmanism
Cut out a set of cards. Half the cards show the names of weather conditions and the other half show the matching pictures. The cards are placed face down and children turn over two to see if they match. Matched pairs are collected until all the cards have gone.

7 Weather leisure
Make displays with titles such as 'When it snows we can...' or 'On windy days we can...', followed by pictures with labels of activities suitable for that weather condition. Extend this to include sports and hobbies that take place in countries with different climates.

3 Weather station
Turn your home corner into a weather station. Here children can keep weather symbols, prepare weather charts from daily readings, make weather forecasts as announcers and design and build their own instruments for recording the weather.

4 Representing the weather
The large wall display above shows how some young children have represented the weather, using tubes for rays of sun and cotton reel prints for clouds. Collections of coloured beads, seeds, pasta or stained sawdust can produce colourful rainbows.

5 Story sticks
Get the children to paint some weather symbols or pictures of places and different types of weather. Cut out the symbols and fix them on to gardening canes or light sticks. Working in groups, the children then create a story that involves the symbols. The children hold up their sticks as they say their piece.

Rain

1 Rain affects people

Talk about the way that rain affects different people. Divide a page into two columns with the headings 'advantages' and 'disadvantages'. Put a title at the top such as 'I am a farmer/builder/post office worker' and complete the list.

2 Rain mobile

If you are not superstitious, hang an umbrella from the ceiling. Alternatively you could use a PE hoop. Create a mobile by adding raindrops and wet weather clothing. Ask the children to add rainy weather words such as 'wet', 'damp' and 'drizzle'.

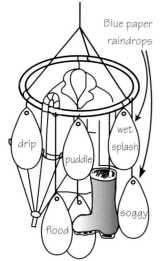

Blue paper raindrops

drip   wet   splash

puddle

flood   soggy

3 Showers

Teach the children the rhyme *Incey Wincey Spider*. Get them to make a series of drawings to show how the weather changes in the rhyme from sun to showers. Display the work by adding clocks to show the time.

rain

We painted on wet pap[er]

rain-hat

boots   raincoat

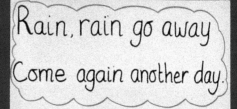

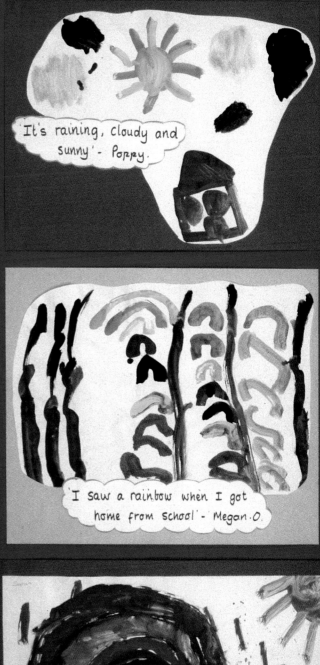

4 Wet weather

Make a display of paintings showing fog, rain, storms and other types of wet weather. Ask the children to add a sentence expressing their feelings about the different weather conditions. What type of weather do they like most?

5 Puddle contours

Wait for a dry or sunny day and tip a can of water on to the playground to make a large puddle. Draw around the edge of the puddle with chalk. As the water evaporates draw around it again and again, making a contour map of the puddle. Discuss what has happened to the water.

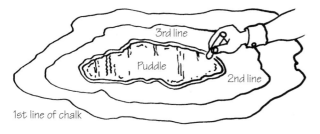

6 Draining away

How does your school keep out the rain? Talk about the way rain falls on the roof, runs down gutter pipes and disappears into drains. Make a survey of things the children can see around the playground that help the rain to drain away.

7 No rain this term

Divide the children into groups. Each group studies one part of the school grounds and reports back on how it would be affected by lack of rain. Write an article for a local newspaper headed 'Pupils record no rain this term'.

8 Research a desert

Organise a project on the deserts of the world. Divide the children into groups and ask each group to investigate a different desert using these questions: Where is it? What is the weather like? Who and what lives there? How do the people, plants and creatures adapt to the desert conditions? What is special or interesting about it? When each group has completed its research, it should put up a small display on its findings.

Weather

Wind

1 Blow, wind, blow

The children designed and made small tissue paper kites for the display below. These models could be part of a design and technology project or could act as the stimulus for creative writing.

2 The north wind and the sun

The north wind and the sun have a competition to see which of them can get a man to take off or put on his coat. Use this story for drama role-playing with props from the dressing-up box. Older children can find out where the north wind comes from and suggest why it is cold.

3 Word ladder

Brainstorm all the words we use to describe the wind. Sequence them on a ladder picture, one word per rung, with least wind at the bottom and strongest wind at the top. Words could include: 'breeze', 'gale', 'storm', and 'calm'.

4 Wind rose

Record the direction of the wind each day on a wind rose and study any pattern that emerges. Which are the prevailing winds in your area? Do they bring particular types of weather?

5 Harnessing the wind

We use the wind for many things - sailing, working windmills, generating electricity and drying clothes. Ask groups of children to conduct research for a report to the rest of the class.

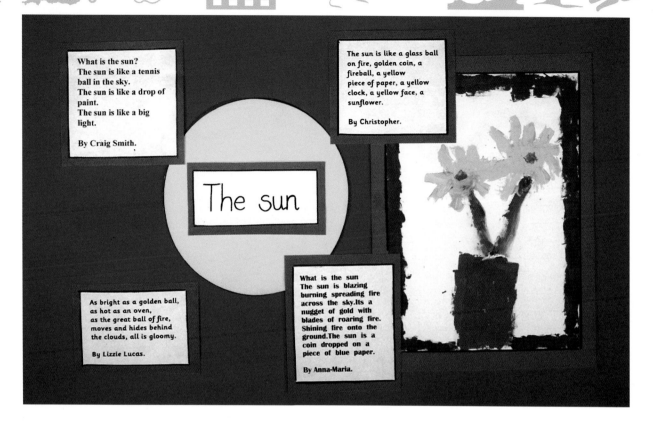

The display shows "The sun" with the following poems:

What is the sun?
The sun is like a tennis ball in the sky.
The sun is like a drop of paint.
The sun is like a big light.

By Craig Smith.

The sun is like a glass ball on fire, golden coin, a fireball, a yellow piece of paper, a yellow clock, a yellow face, a sunflower.

By Christopher.

As bright as a golden ball, as hot as an oven, as the great ball of fire, moves and hides behind the clouds, all is gloomy.

By Lizzie Lucas.

What is the sun The sun is blazing burning spreading fire across the sky.Its a nugget of gold with blades of roaring fire. Shining fire onto the ground.The sun is a coin dropped on a piece of blue paper.

By Anna-Maria.

Sun

1 Feeling the heat

Identify the areas of your school that are normally hot and sunny at the middle of the day. Are there any areas that are shady and cool? Use a thermometer to record the differences in temperature and display the results on a map or a plan.

2 Sunny places

Working from a newspaper, make a list of cities around the world that have sunny weather. Find these places on a map of the world and add a sunshine symbol next to each one. Older children could record the temperature and discuss why some places are hotter than others.

3 Sun poems

In the display above, children have written their sun poems on a computer, printed them out, and put them next to a sunflower painting inspired by Van Gogh's masterpiece.

4 *The Sun Has Got His Hat On*

This song typifies the way we feel in sunny weather. Children could compose their own songs for other types of weather.

The sun has got his hat on,
Hip- hip- hip- hoo- -ray The sun has got his
hat on, and he's com- ing out to- day.

Snow and ice

1 Jack Frost

Jack Frost personifies icy weather. In the display above he is made from triangles of silver foil and surrounded by a collage of children's pictures showing different interpretations of a frosty morning.

2 Likes and dislikes

Children can make a chart to shows their likes and dislikes of snowy weather. Extend the survey by asking people of different generations with different jobs for their opinions too. Are there any patterns that emerge?

3 Cold weather

Make a class collection of newspaper articles about cold weather and the problems it causes. Children could add their own commentary about the difficulties experienced by people, plants and animals.

4 Winter gallery

The display below shows different aspects of cold weather. On the left, the dangers of ice are illustrated by the pictures of a crashed car and the footprints disappearing into the frozen pond. In the middle, the snowman indicates how snowy weather can be fun. On the right, the Christmas cards and landscape paintings show how artists have responded to wintry conditions.

5 Cold places

Read the class the story of Scott's voyage to Antarctica. Then the children make and display models of Antarctic animals, snowmobiles, aircraft with skis, scientists with thermal clothing, ice-breaking ships and ice floes made from polystyrene.

6 Winter weather

Children stick today's date on a chart of different weather pictures (see right).

7 Comparisons

Get the children to find out about everyday life in a cold place. Divide a large sheet of paper into two columns. In the first column, children record information about their own environment. In the second, they show what they have discovered about the place they are studying. Suitable topics to consider include: houses, food, clothes and wildlife.

13

Weather

Recording the weather

1 Rain gauge

Cut off and invert the top of a plastic bottle to make a rain gauge. After trying it out during rainy weather, devise a scale you can use with it. Do all parts of the school grounds receive the same amount of rain?

2 Wind vanes

Look for wind vanes on churches and other high buildings. Now get the children to make their own wind vanes and test them to see how well they work. The simplest design is a paper arrow attached to a stick.

3 Wind strength

Older children can measure the wind strength by suspending balsa wood bars from a frame to see how the wind changes in strength. They could devise their own version of the Beaufort scale to correspond with the number of bars that move.

4 World weather

Collect weather reports from around the world from newspapers and travel guides. Use the reports to make hand-drawn or computer-generated graphs and written reports of the weather over a period of a week. Decorate the work with weather symbols and display around a world map. Younger children can take their nearest city and compare its weather with one other place in the world.

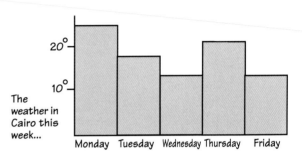

The weather in Cairo this week...

Word bank

chart
compass
direction
rain gauge
temperature
thermometer
wind vane

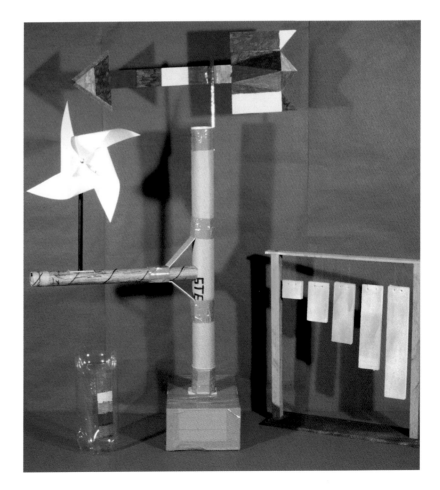

5 Keeping records

You can keep a simple record of weather conditions using symbols on a chart. Alternatively you could use a computer program such as *Weather Mapper* (TAG Developments). This helps with making comparisons and seeing trends and patterns.

light rain   heavy rain

thunder   sunny

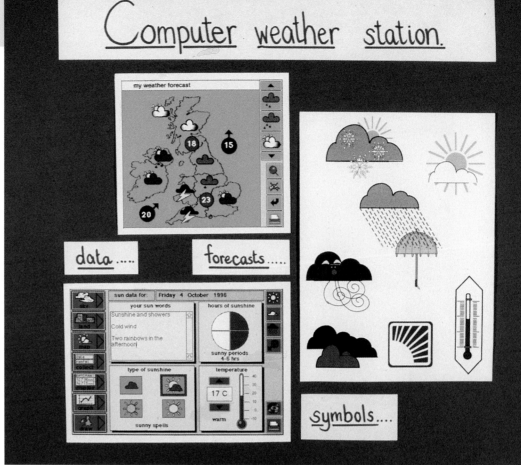

Computer weather station.

data ....   forecasts ....

symbols ....

Teaching plan

Enquiry question	Learning objective	Pupil activities
Is the weather the same everywhere in the world?	Weather varies across the UK and world.	• UK and world weather map work • Weather forecast play activities
What types of weather are there?	There are all types of weather through the year.	• Weather recording • Wind rose and word ladder • Art activities for different weather conditions
How does the weather affect us?	We adapt our lives to fit in with weather changes.	• Winter hazards • Using the wind • Songs and stories • Leisure in different weather

Different seasons

1 Seasons map

Take your class on a walk in each of the four seasons. Talk about the sights, sounds and smells, make drawings, collect nature specimens and take photographs. Display the photographs and pictures around a large-scale local map. Keep the four maps and compare the seasonal variations at the end of the year.

2 Seasons tree

The model tree above is made from a tube of chicken wire, covered in papier mâché or Modroc. The branches are made from rolls of newspaper taped around an old umbrella frame. Use painted cocktail sticks stuck into Plasticine for the hedgehog and playdough for the fruit.

Word bank

autumn
change
harvest
migration
pattern
spring
summer
weather
winter

3 Winter picture

The display below uses a grey background and bare trees to give a real feeling of coldness. The trees are simply cut out of black sugar paper and have scribbled white crayon on them to hint at snow on the bark. The warm browns and red of the house emphasise the feeling of cosiness.

4 Add to the display

After a few weeks ask the children to think of ways to change the winter picture, e.g. by adding a group of brightly dressed children building a snowman. Later on remove the brightly dressed children and add animals that are out and about in the winter.

5 Change the season

When spring comes ask the children to alter the picture to show landscape changes. Enquiry questions include: Which plants flower first? What happens in the pond during spring?

6 Seasonal migration

Find out about a bird, insect or animal that migrates. Draw arrows on a map to show the journeys it makes, labelling each arrow with the appropriate season. Add silhouette shapes of the creature and a sentence saying why it migrates.

7 Alpine pastures

In the Alps and other mountainous regions farmers move herds of animals to summer pastures as the weather gets warmer. Make contrasting pictures of an alpine meadow in summer and winter. Swiss and Austrian travel brochures are useful resources. Read passages from *Heidi* by Johanna Spyri.

8 Nomads

People who lived in deserts traditionally moved from place to place to find food and water. Children can research one group of people suggesting how modern conveniences lessen the need for migration.

Around the year

1 Autumn display

Take an autumn walk to collect fruit from trees and hedgerows such as acorns, hazelnuts and chestnuts. Each group makes a display case from small boxes. Add fruits and label.

acorns
chestnuts
Autumn fruits
ash keys
The school field October

2 Winter scene

Brainstorm words or phrases that describe the effects of winter on people and the environment. Use circles of white paper and snip along the folds to make snowflakes. Then glue chosen phrases to the centres to make a display.

Seasons

3 Seasonal portrait

For a single season, children research temperatures, rainfall, length of days, pastimes, animal activities, trees and flowers, holidays, festivals, and school events. Set the information out in columns under headings so that another season can be added as the year progresses. Seasons can easily be compared this way.

4 Seasonal clothes

Divide the children into four groups. Ask each group to bring into school a set of clothes, a photo of people and a country picture for the season they have been allocated. Each group makes its own display for others to guess the season.

5 Seasons tower

Make a cardboard tower and decorate each side with symbols or pictures representing a different season. Older children could add cut-out figures of four people with joined hands, dressed for the different seasons. Join the figures in a circle and place around the tower, matching clothing with season.

6 Seasonal jobs

Make a questionnaire to give to a local business such as a hotel, an ice-cream shop, a farm, a coach company, or a road haulage company with questions about how their trade changes through the year. Record the changes on a seasons wheel.

7 Wet and dry seasons

India and other tropical countries have a wet season and a dry season. Get the children to draw seasonal dials to show this weather pattern. Talk about what it might be like to live there and list the advantages and disadvantages.

8 Seasons in New Zealand

Find out about a country in the southern hemisphere such as New Zealand where it is summer when it is winter in Britain. The children can write a diary showing seasonal events, e.g. 'In December it is summer so we go to the beach'.

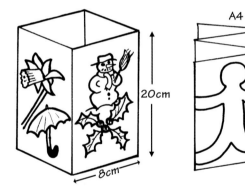

Teaching plan

Enquiry question	Learning objective	Pupil activities
What are the different seasons?	In Britain there are four seasons, each with distinctive weather.	• Painting and models • Seasonal dials
How do the seasons affect people, plants and creatures?	People adapt their clothes and work. There is a pattern to animal and plant life.	• Seasonal walks and displays • Migration of animals
Are the seasons the same everywhere?	Some countries have a different pattern of seasons.	• Wet and dry seasons • Seasons in New Zealand

Water

River features

1 Journey of a river

Children can build this display in sections. Begin with the mountains, then show how the water collects in streams and lakes, flows downhill through gorges and waterfalls and reaches the sea in an estuary. Details of the countryside, riverside towns and ports can be added afterwards. Keep a set of labels in a box or pocket so children can add them to the display to test their knowledge of river words.

2 River dictionary

Make a class book giving definitions and pictures of features along a river's course.

Focus

- River features
- Erosion and deposition
- Water cycle
- Saving water
- Using IT

Word bank

bank
estuary
gorge
lake
mouth
reservoir
source
stream
tributary
valley
waterfall

3 Using rivers

Follow the course of a river on a map of your area and list the different ways in which it is used. For example, rivers provide power for dams; they cut valleys to make routes for roads and railways; they create fertile lowlands where we can grow crops and build towns.

All rivers lead to the sea.

Animals enjoy the river.

Rivers are used for many activities

Rafting on the river

4 Data handling

Use a data handling program to create a river datafile. Record the name of the river, where it rises, the sea or ocean it flows into, its length, and the main cities on its banks. You could use the datafile in a display and add pictures of rivers from an encyclopedia program such as *Encarta*.

5 Water cycle

Set up a diagrammatic display to show the water cycle. You could either build this up in stages as you explain the process or use the complete display to introduce the topic. Remove the labels and ask children to make their own diagrams as an assessment activity.

6 Evaporation

Fill some shallow dishes with water and leave them around your school. Record how long the water takes to evaporate. Include places that are warm, cold, damp and draughty to obtain a range of results.

The vapour rises and cools, it turns back into water.

The water evaporates and rises into the air as water vapour.

Water falls as rain or snow.

The sun heats the water in seas, lakes, rivers and on the land.

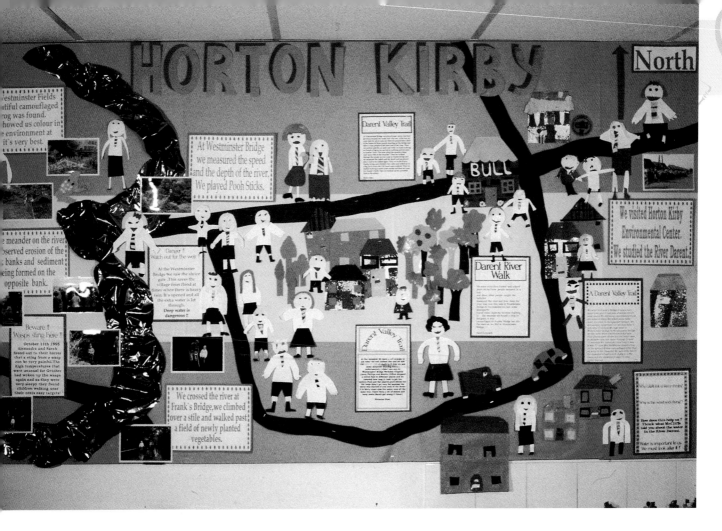

River visits

1 Fieldwork

Make a visit to a stream or river in your area. Walk along the bank and get the children to take photographs of the things they notice. You could focus on plants and creatures, how people use the water or the course that the river takes.

2 River depth

Choosing a safe place, measure the depth of a stream with metre sticks. Is the water the same depth at other places upstream and downstream?

3 River plan

Make a plan of a small section of stream, looking for evidence of erosion (undercutting), deposition (banks of sand or mud), speed and direction of flow. A stream can show all the features of a river system in miniature. Is there any material being carried by the water? Drop 'Pooh sticks' into the middle to assess the speed of movement. Does the water flow faster in some places than in others?

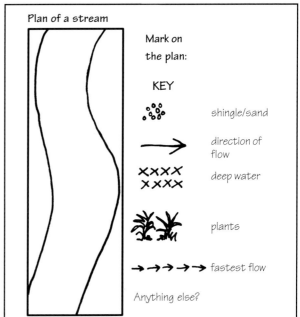

4 River frieze

Use an aerial photograph or map to make a drawing or display of a river in your area. Add notes describing any special features such as waterfalls and reservoirs. Compare the river at different points along its journey.

5 River model

Make a model in a box of a fish's eye view of a river, showing the shape of banks, deposits of mud and different plants and creatures.

6 Pond life

Make a cross-section picture showing the plants that live at different depths in a pond. Use overlapping circles of brown tissue paper to represent the soil and cover the water with pink-tinted Cellophane to create an underwater effect.

7 River stories

Read *Mr Gumpy's Outing* by John Burningham (Puffin 1978) to the class. Ask the children to draw their own picture maps of the journey in the boat. They can also add river features such as sandbanks, shallows and pools.

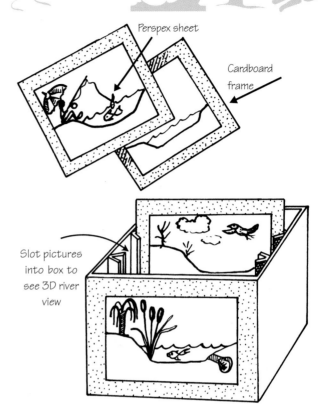

Perspex sheet

Cardboard frame

Slot pictures into box to see 3D river view

POND PLANTS

water iris

duckweed

water lily

reedmace

Canadian Pondweed

Water

Using water

1 Water survey
Get the children to make a survey of the number of times they use water for drinking, washing, flushing the toilet and other activities during a day. Record the results on hand-drawn or computer-generated charts. Why is water so important in our lives?

2 Saving water
Discuss different ways of saving water in school. Examples include installing toilets with small cisterns, using taps that turn off automatically and saving rainwater from the roof to water the grounds. Write a code for saving water.

we use water for...

drinking

growing things

cleaning things

having a bath

flushing the toilet

having a shower

cooking, drinking, washing up

3 Water diary

Keep a class water diary. Children record in words and pictures how they or their family use water. Each entry should record a different way of using water.

4 Reservoirs

Read the story *Shaker Lane* by Alice Provensen (Walker 1987). Why are reservoirs needed? Who benefits from them? Are there any disadvantages? Working from a map, make a list of reservoirs in your region. Decide on a suitable place for a new reservoir and set up a simulation to debate the issues that might arise from the scheme.

This was a quiet valley before the reservoir was built...

Look at how many times we used water on 29th April.

Bar Chart

Pie Chart
- TOILET
- WASH HANDS
- CLASS SINK
- DRINK

How can we save water?

5 Canal life

Geography and history can be combined in a school visit to a canal. Children can find out why canals were built, how canals were used in the past and how they are used now.

6 Canal research

Look at a map of your area to see if there are any canals. How does the canal manage to cross hills and valleys? Locate the locks, tunnels and bridges. Create a wall map as part of a display. Add information boxes around the edge saying why the canal was built, what it was used for in the past, how people use it today, and so on.

Teaching plan

Enquiry question	Learning objective	Pupil activities
What course do rivers take?	Knowledge of the features of a river system.	• Place labels on a display • Make a river dictionary • River database
How do rivers shape the landscape?	Rivers flow at different speeds, eroding and depositing material.	• Fieldwork investigations • River plans and models
Why is water an important resource?	We use water for drinking and washing.	• Surveys of water use • Research and discussion

Types of home

1 Model houses

Make some model houses from light card. Add coloured paper squares for the roof tiles and rubbings of materials for other surfaces. You can arrange the models to show the pattern of streets and houses in your local area, or you could construct a village scene. There are also possibilities for creating journeys using directional vocabulary.

2 Building materials

Set up a display of building materials such as brick, slate, tile and wood. Provide the children with a set of labels in a box so they can test that they know which is which. Get the children to weigh and measure each item as part of their work in science and maths.

Focus

- Local fieldwork
- Housing
- Character of places
- Models and charts

3 Patterns and decorations

Plan a short walk in your neighbourhood to look for patterns and decorations. As well as noticing the shapes of roof tiles, brick courses and window panes, get the children to look for architectural details. Ridge tiles, bargeboards, ironwork and front paths often contain interesting patterns. Develop work on tessellation and geometric shapes when you return to the classroom.

Homes and streets

4 Sell your house

Ask each child to make an estate agent's advertisement, using a picture and description of his or her own house. Older children could include internal plans. Display the adverts on a board entitled 'Property for Sale'.

5 Semi-detached origami

Make some origami house models (see below). Ask the children to show who or what is inside when they do the decorations. Use the display to demonstrate house numbering, either sequential or odd and even.

6 My house

Make a display of photographs or paintings of children's homes around a map of your local area with your school in the centre. Divide the map into north, east, south and west. Label with ' We live north of the school' and so on.

7 Who lives here?

A class made the display below of famous homes around the world and included their teacher's home, which is called *Shanti* - this is a Hindi word meaning 'peaceful haven'.

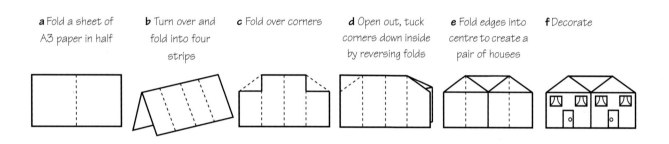

a Fold a sheet of A3 paper in half   **b** Turn over and fold into four strips   **c** Fold over corners   **d** Open out, tuck corners down inside by reversing folds   **e** Fold edges into centre to create a pair of houses   **f** Decorate

The Street Detectives hunted for clues to find out about Park Road. Read their investigation reports to find out more.

Our street

1 My street

Make imitation street name plates for your area. Get the children to add paintings of faces or people they know so that each street has a gallery of inhabitants. Older children can combine this with the next activity.

2 Street study

Select two or three streets around your school that each have a different character. Start with a survey of features such as trees, bins, pavements, bus stop, flats, bungalows. Display the information as a mobile, hanging symbols below the street name plate. Discuss the questions of noise and pollution in the street.

Word bank

bungalow
detached
flat
mobile home
services
street furniture
terrace
trail

3 Park Road

The children who created the display on page 28 visited a local road in the guise of 'street detectives'. They made detailed observations of the houses, street furniture and decorations, and recorded what they saw in a trail booklet.

4 Street names

Use a local street map to find street names with a meaning, e.g. Mill Lane, Market Street. Make a display that shows how children imagined the street was when it was named. Can local people help your research, or can your local council tell you how names for a new housing estate are chosen?

5 Different designs

Talk about different house designs - detached, semi-detached, terrace, flat, bungalow and mobile home. The children could record what they see in the local area, using tick sheets, drawings or photographs. You could also make prints as an artwork exercise. The photograph on the right shows a lino print of a converted oast house in Kent.

6 Pipes and wires

Rubbings made in the local streets with chunky wax crayons make a striking wall display. Choose different colours for different types of services such as blue for water, red for heating/cooking and purple for communications. Use a computer to draw a variety of bar charts and graphs. Stress the usual safety procedures when working out of doors and never allow the children to make rubbings in the road.

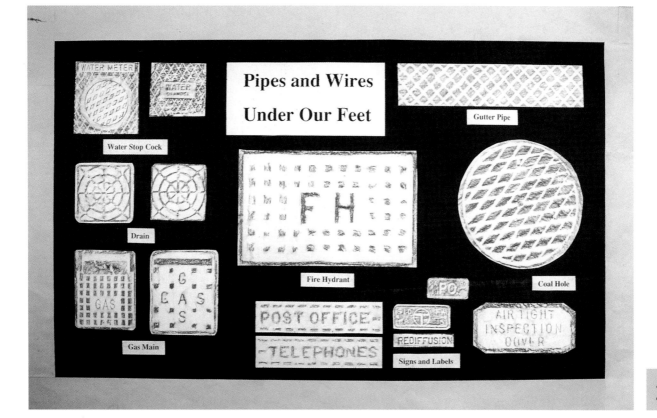

Homes and streets

Addresses

1 Whose front door?

Children make pictures of front doors that open out (see right). They add fittings to make each door individual - letterbox, bell, number, windows and so on. The children then draw family portraits inside. The class could play a guessing game about who they think lives behind each door.

2 Front door colours

Observe and record the colours of the front doors in a nearby street. Display the results as a bar chart or pictogram with little coloured drawings. Which colours are the most popular?

3 My address

Get the children to bring a teddy or favourite toy animal to school for a day. Ask them to add a label around the neck saying 'If found, please return to …' The children should then add their own name and address.

4 Mapping my address

Children make a series of maps with each map showing one of the following: their house; their street; their town; the UK; Europe; the world. They mark their position on each one.

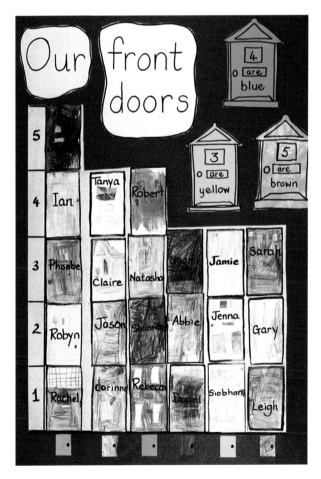

30

Homes from Wind in the Willows

5 Homes in stories

The Wind in the Willows is a story that mentions many different homes. In the display above, the children have made drawings of where the characters live. Questions about the need for shelter and about how animals survive in the wild arise naturally from this work.

6 Why move house?

Start a discussion on the reasons why people move house. Then give the children a survey sheet to take home to discover how many times their parents have moved. Older children can plot their family origins on a map of the region, the UK or the world.

Teaching plan

Enquiry question	Learning objective	Pupil activities
Are all homes the same?	There are different types of homes in the local area and abroad.	• Environmental walk • Models and prints
What can we learn about streets near our school?	Each street has its own character.	• Surveys and detective work • Street furniture and rubbings
What is my address?	I know my address.	• Front door studies • Animal addresses • Homes in stories

School grounds

Around your school

1 Know your school

This quiz was made by a head teacher for the whole school to use. Children found the things in the photographs and marked them on a map of the school grounds. Older children could make their own quiz for another class to try. They could also look for clues of historical change.

Focus

- Attractive and unattractive places
- Improving the environment
- Maps and directions
- Site conditions

Word bank

attractive
compass
direction
environment
habitat
landscape
orienteering
plan
signpost
wildlife

School features quiz.

Mark these on your map.

What are the
Where would you find them

2 Different places

Make a list of different places in and around your school. Which ones do the children like visiting? Where do they play games? Are there any places that are daunting? Record the children's impressions, using notes and pictures around a large-scale map of your school.

3 Orienteering

Use the photographs in the quiz to make an orienteering game. Starting at a control centre, give the children cards with directional instructions, e.g. 'Go south to find feature number six'. When they arrive at the feature, the children find a stamp and pad to mark their card. They then return to the control centre and do the next task until they have a complete set of stamped cards.

4 NESW

Paint or construct a compass in your playground showing the directions of north, east, south and west. Use the compass points as gathering points for children during a games lesson, e.g. 'Run to the east corner when I blow the whistle'.

5 Landscape views

Work in an open area and get the children to produce landscape sketches showing what they can see in four directions. Display the work around a large-scale map of the area. Older children could focus on eight compass points.

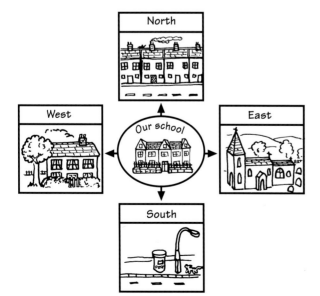

6 Signposts

Make a signpost by attaching arrows and labels to a pole and stand from the PE apparatus. Place the signpost in the playground to point to features you can see. Using local knowledge, progress to features further afield. Then extend the work to more distant places with information gleaned from a map.

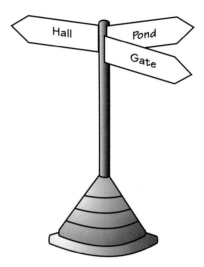

7 Services

Look around the school grounds for evidence of services that the school uses. Ways of representing these services include:
- making rubbings, e.g. of manhole covers;
- sketching, e.g. of telephone wires;
- taking photographs, e.g. of school meals arriving;
- making a log, e.g. of the time the postman and milkman call.

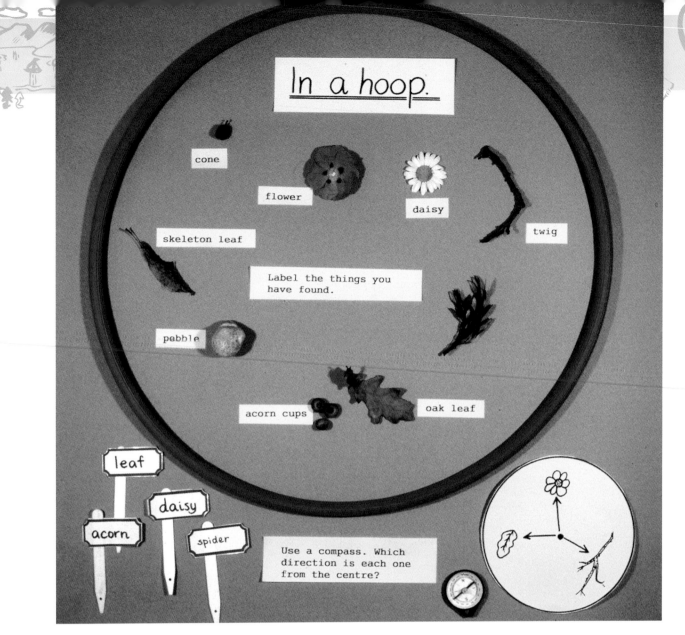

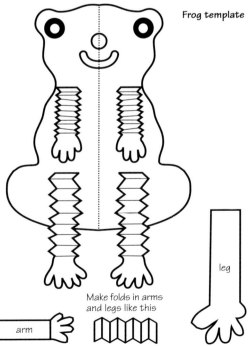

Frog template

The nature garden

1 In a hoop

Place a hoop on a piece of grass or a flowerbed or hang it on an old wall or fence. List the things inside the hoop and show their positions. Compare what you find in the open, under a hedge, and alongside a building. Is there any evidence that plants and creatures are affected by localised weather conditions?

2 Summer in the wildlife garden

Observe the pond life, butterflies and flowers in the wildlife garden. Back in school you can create a collage to show this environment. Use paper plates for mini ponds and get the children to add plants and creatures. Frogs with concertina legs can be made from paper.

Make folds in arms and legs like this

arm

leg

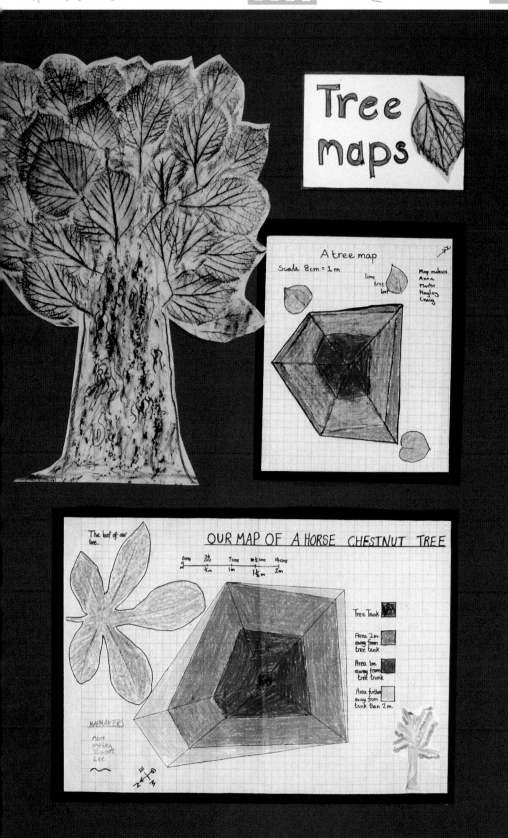

3 Map a tree

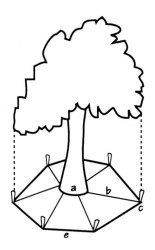

a Tie a piece of string around the tree trunk near the ground.

b Walk out from the trunk until you are under the furthest twig.

c Put a stick in the ground, joining the stick to the tree with string.

d Repeat this all around the tree, at least eight times.

e Link all the sticks together around the outside with another piece of string.

f Measure each radial string and decide on a scale, e.g. 1cm on paper = 50cm on the ground.

g Draw the tree plan on squared paper, using a compass to get each direction as accurate as possible.

Improvement ideas

1 Litter monsters
Young children can collect old boxes and make them into monster litter bins. The mouth provides a slit for rubbish to be put into. The bin is decorated with materials from the art box.

2 Notice board
Get the children to design a notice board to tell everyone what is happening in your school grounds. The board will need a title and a border and a space in the middle for an A4-size sheet of paper (see top right).

3 Painted pebbles
Using acrylic paints and varnish, the children can decorate large smooth pebbles with butterflies or flowers. A pile of these pebbles looks colourful at the base of a notice board or bird table, or around a flower border.

4 Bird plaques
Make plaques showing the birds you can find in your area. Use squares of seasoned wood for the base. Help the children to draw the outlines by photocopying and enlarging pictures for them. Colour the plaques with acrylic paints and fix them to the playground fence as a frieze.

School Path Designs

5 Design a path

A class was asked to design a patterned path to make a part of their school more attractive. The photograph above shows some of their ideas.

6 School signs

Children can help to design and paint the notices needed in the school grounds to direct and inform visitors.

Teaching plan

Enquiry question	Learning objective	Pupil activities
How can we get to know our school grounds better?	Close observation of school buildings and environment.	• Direction games and sketches • Features quiz • Tree maps and hoop quadrants
How can we improve our school grounds?	We can all help to make and keep the school attractive.	• Design small-scale improvements • Make notices, signs and plaques • Litter monsters

Jobs

People who help us

Focus

- Different types of work
- Provision of goods and services

1 Services

Children write to or contact people who work in school (cleaner, caretaker, painter and so on) inviting them to talk about their job. Record the results in a class book, using drawings, questionnaires and written descriptions.

2 Safety

Set up a display of protective clothing and equipment that people use in their jobs. Ask the children to make posters in the shape of a protective item with warnings or information inside the shape.

Word bank

harbour
job
lifeboat
safety
services
timetable
uniform

3 Uniforms

Working in groups, the children find out about jobs where people have to wear uniforms. What is the uniform like and why is it needed? Make models from cardboard boxes to show the different people. Each group can then present its model to the rest of the class and say a few words about 'My day as a ...'

4 Timetables

Find out how different people spend their working day. Get the children to draw clocks to show what different people are doing at specific times. Make comparisons with your own class routine and display the work on a timeline.

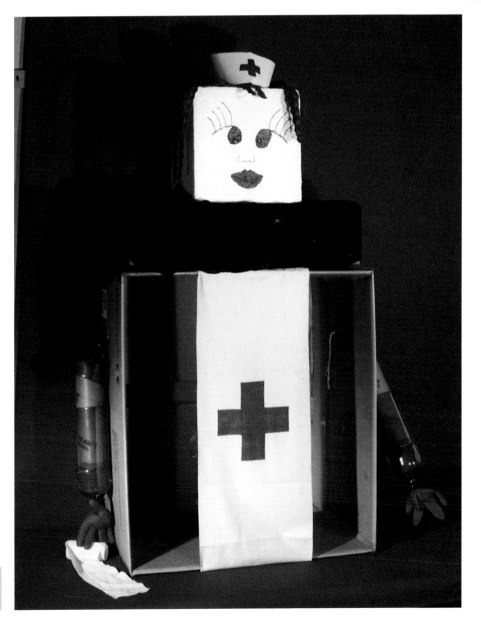

Fishing and harbours

1 The fish stall

Some old netting and sea shells can transform
the home corner or shop corner into a fish stall.
Children can make playdough fish and their own
advertisement posters. Decorate the wall behind
the stall with an underwater scene or harbour
picture to fit in with a seashore theme.

2 Harbour jobs

Brainstorm with your class the jobs that take
place around a harbour. Get the children to draw
people involved in their trade such as a
fisherman on a boat, a person mending nets, the
harbour master in an office and a vendor at an
ice-cream kiosk.

3 Danger at sea

The dangers of being at sea can be introduced
by a story such as *The Mousehole Cat* by
Antonia Barber (Walker 1990). Research into
lifeboats and famous rescues provides a natural
follow-up.

4 Building harbours

Why do people build harbours? Children can
look at photographs and postcards and draw
aerial views to show how the shape of a harbour
keeps the rough sea out.

5 Star-gazey pies

Make a cheese pastry mixture with 500g plain
flour, 250g butter and 250g grated cheese. Add
an egg yolk and some milk and roll out into
strips about 8cm wide and 12cm long. Wrap
each strip around a sardine, leaving the head
peeping out. Moisten and stick down the edges,
brush with milk and cook for 10 minutes
at 200°C.

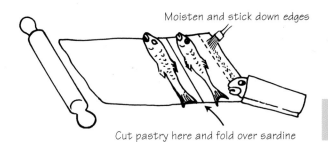

Moisten and stick down edges

Cut pastry here and fold over sardine

The postal service

1 Katie Morag

Use *Katie Morag Delivers the Mail* by Mairi Hedderwick (Picture Lions 1986) as the stimulus for some work on the postal service:

a Finding the way
Working from the pictures in the book, make a list of the things Katie Morag passed on her way to each house. Use this list to make a simple route map to help her find her way again.

b Post office drama
Select one person from the story and discuss when he or she would use the post office. Make a role-play about this person's visit. Is he or she handing something in (letter, parcel) or is he or she taking something away (stamps, pension money)? Talk about the inputs and outputs.

c Postcards
Take on the identity of a holidaymaker visiting the Isle of Struay. Design a postcard that he or she might send to show what the island's scenery, buildings and wildlife are like.

d Souvenirs
The holiday children have found some pictures and other things to show their friends at school. What would you bring back from Struay? (Get the class to mock up a display using Plasticine or playdough for artefacts.)

2 Addresses

Ask the children to send themselves a postcard showing one of the jobs in the postal service. Get them to design a label for their school bag with their address and postcode on it.

3 Postboxes

Visit a postbox near your school. Record information on collection times. Look at the crest and lock. What stops the rain running into the letter box? Use these observations to make a life-size cut-out of a postbox in your classroom. The children could also make individual postboxes of their own with stamps and addresses glued on to them as decoration.

4 Stamps

Use a collection of stamps and postmarks from around the world or the UK to create an interactive display where the children match each place to its location with the help of an atlas (see right).

Word bank

address
delivery
input
output
postbox
route
stamp

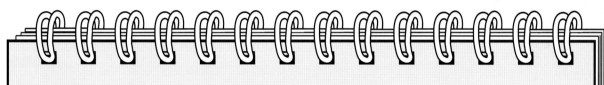

Teaching plan

Enquiry question	Learning objective	Pupil activities
What different kinds of work do people do?	Some people provide services to help us.	• Survey of jobs around school • Uniforms and safety equipment
What jobs do people do at a harbour?	People work on fishing boats, sell fish and look after visitors.	• Fish stall role-play • Danger at sea • Harbour jobs
How does the post arrive?	The postman knows where people live by their address.	• Story of Katie Morag • Stamps and postmarks

Food and farming

Farm visit

1 Farm visit

Try to visit a farm or invite a farmer into your school to talk about his or her work. The National Farmers' Union may be able to provide a local contact. If this is impossible, write a questionnaire asking all the things you want to know and send it to your local Young Farmers' Club.

Focus

- Farm animals
- Crops
- Land use
- Buying and selling
- Mapmaking

Word bank

countryside
crop
fertiliser
field
harvest
hedge
organic
produce

2 Pigs

After a class visit to a farm, the children each made a pink pig with a paper plate face for the wall display below. They also used a word processor to record what they had learnt about the pigs. Older children could find out the annual jobs on a pig farm and display the work on a flow diagram.

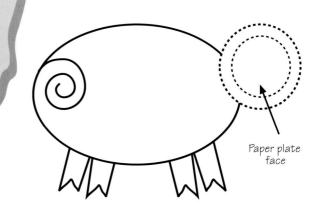

Paper plate face

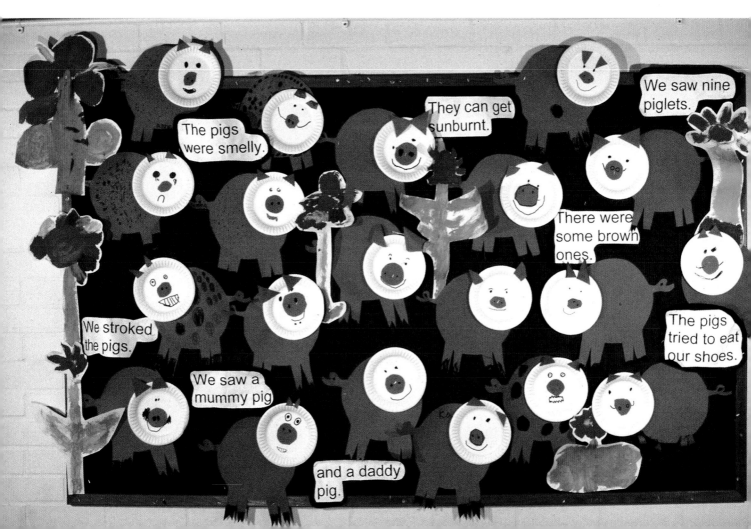

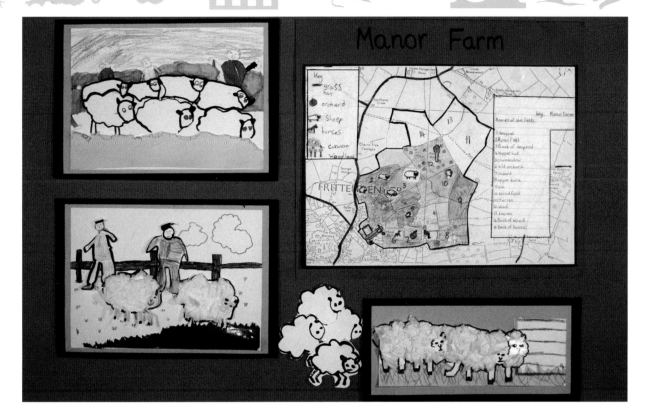

3 Farm portrait

Using a large map and pictures that the children have painted, make a portrait of a farm you have visited. Make sure the pictures include the machines and equipment needed to keep the farm running. If there are animals, you can use a template to create a flock of sheep or a herd of cows. You could also add statistics about the number of animals and the amount of land, and portraits of the people who work on the farm.

4 Checking the boundaries

During the farm visit get the children to walk along the boundary of one of the fields. Look for gaps that sheep could escape through, places where fences or walls need repairing, gates in poor condition and any hazards such as dangerous litter. Record the findings on a simple field plan.

5 Caring for the countryside

Discuss with the children the consequences of leaving empty bottles in the countryside. Now give each child an outline bottle shape and ask the children to draw or write down what happens to their abandoned bottle. You could display the work as bottles standing on a wall.

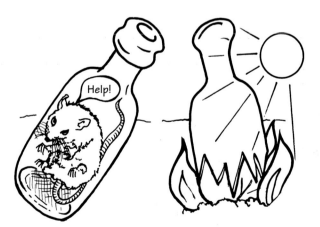

Growing things

1 Fruit and vegetables

Make papier mâché models of different fruits and vegetables. Alternatively, bring some fresh farm produce to school. Arrange the produce in a labelled display.

2 Farm produce

Get the children to paint pictures of farm produce. The children can then sort their paintings into sets, using large hoops placed on the floor. Suitable groupings could include: things that grow below/above ground and dark/light colours.

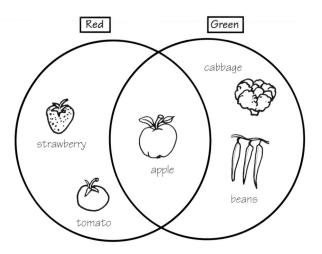

3 Growing crops

Make pictures that show the different stages involved in growing and harvesting particular crops. Display the work as sequence drawings or mobiles. Include information about the weather. You could also add photographs from magazines of the machines that the farmer uses.

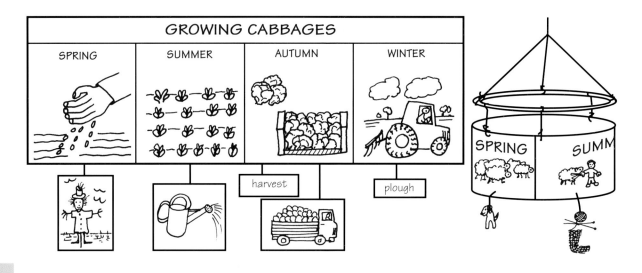

44

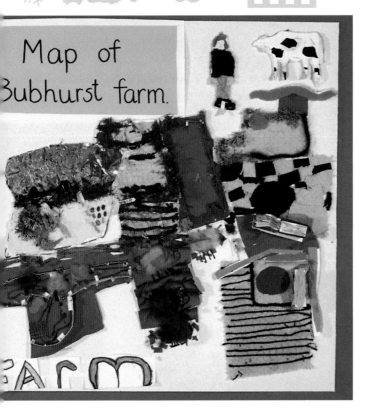

6 Collage map
Divide the children into groups and give them some pieces of fabric and an outline map of a farm they have visited. Using these materials, the children can then create a collage map like the one on the left by selecting a suitable material for each field, cutting out the shape and glueing it on to the map. Use a sheet of cardboard for the base and small boxes for models of the farm buildings. Ponds, hedges and other details will help to make the maps realistic.

7 Organic food
Most supermarkets now sell organic fruit and vegetables. Bring a few sample packets into class and discuss what makes organic produce different. What are the advantages and disadvantages for farmers in growing organic food? After the discussion the children draw pictures of a farmer, a shopkeeper and a customer, each with a speech bubble giving his or her view.

4 Fields
Using a map of a farm you have visited, get the children to colour code the different crops to show how each field is used. If the size of each field is shown, the children should also be able to work out the area devoted to each crop. Display the results in a bar chart and discuss the findings. Why do farmers usually grow more than one crop? Do they use the fields in the same way each year or do they rotate the crops?

5 Over the gate
Children make pictures of a field scene. Then they frame and front the picture with a cut-out gate, which can be opened to reveal the field landscape.

8 Food from the farm
This is an assessment activity. Use paper plates to provide the background for meals that the children create to represent the foods they now recognise as farm produce (see above).

Sheep and wool

1 Made from wool

Set up a display of different things made of wool. The children could each contribute an item and write a label to go with it. Discuss why wool is a suitable material to use in each case.

2 Weaving

Make some weaving cards about 20cm x 15cm from stiff white or black paper (see below). Fold each card loosely in half and cut slits to make seven strips, each 1cm wide, on the 'body'. Now cut four slits of the same size on the 'face'. Use contrasting colour paper for the weaving and complete by adding eyes and nose.

Fold in half and cut slits

3 Keeping warm

Fill two screw-top jars with hot water and measure the temperature of the water. Wrap one of the jars in a cotton scarf and the other in a wool scarf. After an hour measure the temperature of the water again. Decide which material keeps us warmer.

Word bank

dye
fleece
lamb
shepherd
spin
weave

Why wear wool?		
	Wool	Cotton
(clock showing 2:00)	60°C	60°C
(clock showing 3:00)	50°C	44°C

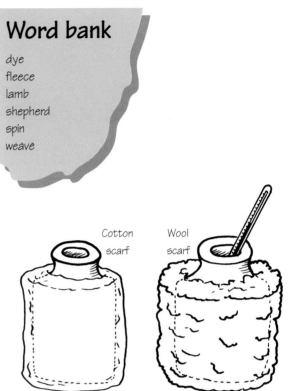

Cotton scarf   Wool scarf

4 Collecting wool

Collect pieces of wool from hedges or fences. Feel the greasiness of the lanolin. Once the wool has been washed it can be dyed. One method is to boil some onion skins in water with a tablespoon of vinegar, allow the water to cool and then soak the wool for half an hour. Try using blackberries or beetroot in the same way.

5 Making wool

Make a series of pictures like the ones below to show how wool is turned into clothes. Include the sheep grazing in fields, the farmer shearing the sheep, the machine spinning the wool in a factory and the clothes on sale in a shop. Add arrows linking each picture to show the sequence.

For extra information, see *Infant Geography Resource Bank* (Stanley Thornes 1994).

Stories and songs

1   In old Amsterdam

A class enhanced its European awareness by making a model of a windmill (see above) and learning the song *The Windmill in Old Amsterdam*. Use corrugated card for the walls of the windmill and strips of blue cardboard from the lining of an apple box for the dyke. Make the mice by slitting the radius of a small circle and the radius of a large circle to form two cones. Join the cones together and add a tail and whiskers.

2   *The Little Red Hen*

The process of turning wheat into bread is clearly explained in *The Little Red Hen*. A version of this familiar story is available from Ladybird Books. Cut up a copy of the book and mount and cover the pictures. Now divide the children into groups and hand out the pictures. Ask each group to say what is happening in its picture, and to work out what will be next in the sequence.

Food and farming

The parable of the sower

3 The parable of the sower

Use an RE link here to reinforce work on growing crops. The quality of the soil is crucial to farmers. Give the children some real poppies and stalks of wheat to study to help them with their artwork. Discuss the different ways in which farmers can prevent weeds growing in fields.

4 *Little Boy Blue*

Make a picture map to show the features in the rhyme *Little Boy Blue*. Discuss why we need to close gates to keep sheep in. Now read the children 'Mr Forgetful' from the *Mr Men* books about a character who forgets there is a sheep loose in the lane.

Teaching plan

Enquiry question	Learning objective	Pupil activities
Why do we need farms?	Farms produce the food we eat.	• Farm portrait • Food from the farm • Organic food
What do farmers do?	Farmers grow crops and keep animals.	• Growing and harvesting • Sequence drawings • Interview and questionnaires
How can we look after the land?	We can all help to keep the country clean.	• Country code • Litter and pollution pictures

Journeys

Going on a journey

1 Rambling

Take the children on a public footpath near your school. The children then make a display of their journey with each child adding a picture of himself or herself in the correct clothing and carrying a rucksack.

Focus

- Trails
- Types of transport
- Directions
- Map work
- Information Technology

Word bank

footpath
journey
route
traffic
trail
transport
vehicle

I LOVE TO GO

A-WANDERING

The Happy Wanderer

I love to go a-wan-der-ing, A— long the moun-tain track, And as I go, I

love to sing, My knap sack on my back —. Val- de ri— Val- de ra— Val- de

ra — Val- de ha ha ha ha ha ha Val de ri—. Val de ra — . My knap sack on my back—.

2 Fill a rucksack

Bring a ready-filled rucksack to school. As it is being unpacked, ask the children to work out the type of journey you have planned. The final clue can always be the map of your destination. Older children can be given cards with details of a proposed journey. They can then decide what will be needed and make an illustrated list or fill the rucksack with items they have collected.

Reservoir walk

A day's hike around a reservoir in the hills. Walkers hope to see buzzards. Ten-mile round trip on footpaths, in autumn.

Night walk

Family go to forest to look for badgers. Three-mile walk, in April.

3 Long distance journeys

Do any of the children's parents work as van or lorry drivers? If so, find out about the places they visit, the loads they carry, and their daily mileage. Ask the drivers to bring back pictures of the places they go to. Display the pictures around a map of the route.

4 Sail the seas

Make a sea frieze. The children draw and cut out pictures of famous or historical ships. They then add cards entitled 'ship's log' giving details of the cargo, routes and other relevant information.

5 Different vehicles

Get the children to make cut-out shapes of vehicles they have travelled in or on. Ask them to fill the empty space inside the shape with details of the journey and the reason why they used that particular method of transport.

6 Transport trees

Discuss the impact of car traffic on people, plants and creatures. Now record the way that children travel to school on a 'transport tree' (see below). Children who walk or cycle add green leaves to the tree as their journey is environmentally friendly. Those who use cars or buses add white leaves. Repeat the survey some weeks later to see if there have been any changes.

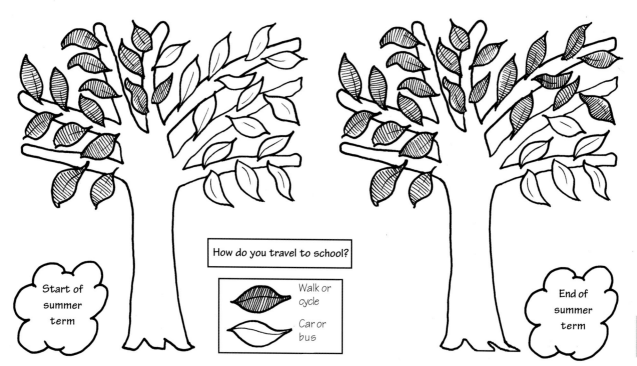

Start of summer term

How do you travel to school?

Walk or cycle

Car or bus

End of summer term

Directions

1 Playmat game

Give the children directions to follow with their toy vehicles on a playmat. You could either use directional words such as 'left' and 'right' or you could challenge the children to find the route to a specific destination such as the park or church. Discuss the landmarks they pass on the way.

2 On the bus

Make a simple picture map like the one below to show a class bus journey. Use labels to indicate directions and to record the features passed on the way. If you protect the labels with a transparent seal and attach them to the display with Velcro, the children can take them off and move them round for reinforcement and assessment activities. Change the landscape after a few weeks by adding some extra buildings and other features. This will ensure you make the most of the display.

3 Footpath trail

Choose a local footpath or create your own circular walk and make a trail for others to follow. Illustrate your trail map with points of interest and landmarks for people to see. This could be developed into a series of walks in your neighbourhood.

4 Sensory trail

A 'talking trail' (the route and landmarks described on a tape) would make your trail accessible to blind people. The children will need to include plenty of things to touch, hear and smell. Pine needles and flowers/leaves of lavender, lemon verbena and geranium plants all give off a powerful scent when crushed.

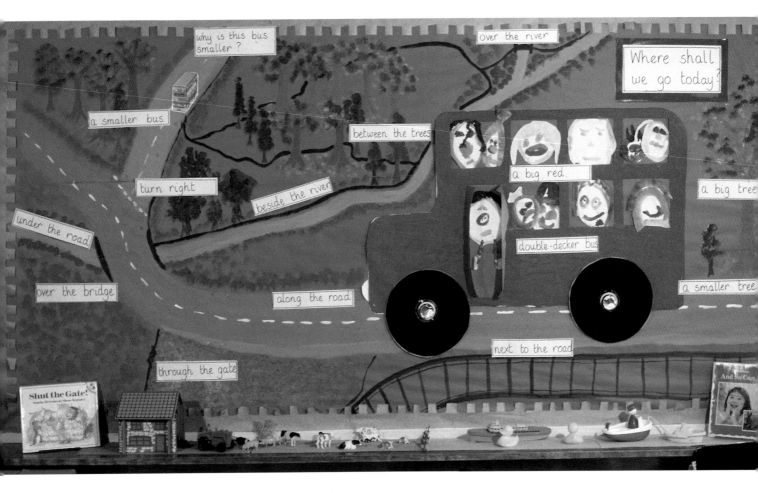

5 The Roamer

Design and make vehicles that can be coupled to a programmable toy and sent on a journey. As well as being an enjoyable exercise in its own right, this will develop links with design and technology.

6 The Turtle

Use a computer program to practise directional vocabulary. The children can trace different routes by moving the cursor across the screen. If they print off their work it can make a lively display and provide a record of different journeys (see right). This also provides direct links with maths shapes work.

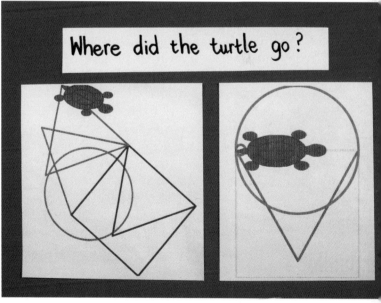

Where did the turtle go?

Journeys

Using stories

1 Myths and fairy tales

Most children will be familiar with fairy tales and enjoy hearing them again. However, many fairy tales can also be used to promote work on routes and journeys. Here are some suggestions:

Hansel and Gretel
What route did the children take through the forest?

Snow White and the Seven Dwarfs
Which places are mentioned in the story?

Theseus and the Minotaur
How did Theseus get out of the maze?

The Emperor's New Clothes
Where did the emperor go on his procession?

Ask the children to draw pictures and maps showing the main features of each story.

2 *Red Riding Hood*

The collage on the right uses lentils, macaroni, straw and other materials to illustrate the *Red Riding Hood* story. The labels and characters are attached with Velcro and can be moved around as the children retell the story to each other. The picture is also divided into grid squares so that the children can use simple grid references to say where each thing can be found. Enquiry questions are another way of focusing the children's attention. For example, the children can discuss which part of the journey was the most dangerous and whether Red Riding Hood could have taken a different route.

3 Red Riding Hood's shopping

Children write a shopping list of gifts to go in Red Riding Hood's basket. Beside each item they write down the type of shop that sells it such as a newsagent, a chemist or a greengrocer.

4 Red Riding Hood's basket

Add letters and numbers to an egg box for grid referencing activities. The children can make Grandma's gifts from playdough or Plasticine and place them in the correct section.

Plasticine gift

Card handle fixed with paper fasteners

Egg carton labelled with grid references

up the hill

along the pa

out of the house

Little Red Riding Hood goes to visit her Grandma. Can you put her journey instructions in the right places?

54

5 *The Hare and the Tortoise*

There are many versions of this story but all involve a race and all mention different landmarks. Get the children to make their own journey map showing the start and the finish and some of the stopping places and diversions along the way. The children could add notes saying why each place is significant.

6 World journeys

Read the children a modern picture book story that involves a world journey such as *Percy Short and Cuthbert* by Susie Jenkin Pearce (Viking 1990) or *The Great Round the World Balloon Race* by Sue Scullard (Macmillan 1993). See if the children can work out the route described by looking at a globe. They could also make drawings of the different places visited.

Teaching plan

Enquiry question	Learning objective	Pupil activities
Why do people make journeys?	Journeys are made for work and leisure.	• Sensory trail
How do people travel?	People use the best type of transport for their journey.	• Different vehicles • Transport trees
How do we give directions?	Knowledge of directional vocabulary.	• On the bus • Playmat game • Computer turtle maps
How do we find our way about?	We follow a route using maps and landmarks.	• The Hare and the Tortoise • World journeys

Maps

Basic skills

1 Plan views

Draw round six everyday objects such as a ruler, a margarine tub or a matchbox. Cut out the shapes, stick them on a sheet of card and see if the children can match each object with its plan. Extend the work by using irregular shapes such as bottles that look different at the top and bottom. You could also get the children to devise some similar puzzles of their own.

2 Overhead projector

Place a coin, a pencil sharpener, a key or a miniature toy on the screen of an overhead projector. Project the image on to a sheet of paper to show the plan view of each item and get the children to draw round the outlines. Cut out the shapes, then colour and label them for a class display. Can the children guess the objects if the labels are removed?

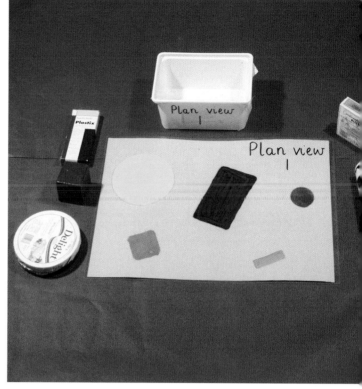

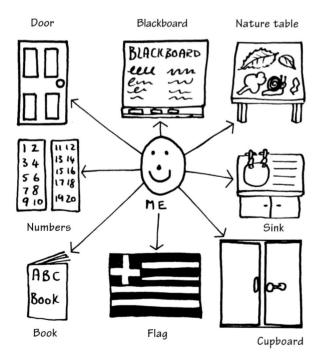

3 Signpost maps

Each child has a sheet of paper. In the middle of their paper the children put a cross or small drawing to show where they sit and then draw arrows pointing to the things around them, indicating what they see in words or pictures. Repeat the activity but get the children to use symbols rather than representational drawings. Older children could pace the distance to the features they have shown. Draw a dotted line down the middle of the page and mark 'left' and 'right'.

4 Reorganising the classroom

Draw a plan of the classroom on a large sheet of card and cover it with a transparent seal. Now give the children pieces of card representing the tables, store cupboards and other furniture. See if the children can arrange the pieces to match the classroom as it is at the moment. Can they rearrange the pieces in a different way? What new item of furniture would they like to have in the classroom and where would they put it?

Word bank

aerial
direction
grid
model
obstacle
plan
scene
sequence

5 Maps from models

Use small models of churches, houses and other buildings to give children the opportunity to create a street or village scene on a sheet of A4 paper. Children draw round the shapes to create a plan and add roads linking different places. They could also add a key and a colour code, e.g. the houses could be shown in yellow and the roads in red.

6 Toy scenes

Ask the children to set up an imaginary scene using toy animals, vehicles or models of household furniture. When they have played for a while, tell the children to record the layout on a piece of paper before they pack the toys away. See if they can re-create the scene from their drawings when they come to school next day. You can use this activity to reinforce previous learning or for assessment.

7 Computer maps

Even young children can create a map on computer showing streets, buildings and other features. *Local Studies* (SoftTeach) is one of a number of suitable programs as it allows

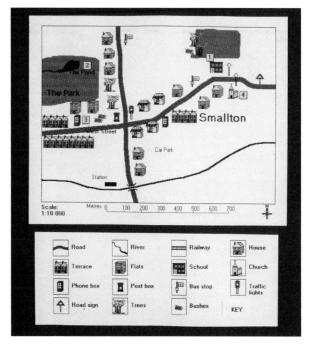

children to use either plans or symbols. There are also opportunities both for generating imaginary maps and for recording actual plans and layouts. Another approach is to give the children a sheet of photocopied symbols and ask them to make their own map by cutting and pasting in a similar way.

57

Maps

Using stories and imagination

1 *Rosie's Walk*

Read the children *Rosie's Walk* by Pat Hutchins (Bodley Head 1962) or another story that involves a journey. Rosie the hen visits the farmyard, pond, haycock, mill, fence and beehives as she is chased by the fox. Give the children a list of features when they draw their maps and check carefully that they have put them in the correct order.

2 *The Three Pigs*

The display below shows differentiated work from *The Three Pigs* story. Each 'map' shows the wolf's route. The simplest version just places the three houses in sequence. The next version includes a route and a number of features. The most sophisticated map contains a wealth of imaginary features, all of which are labelled and shown in realistic locations.

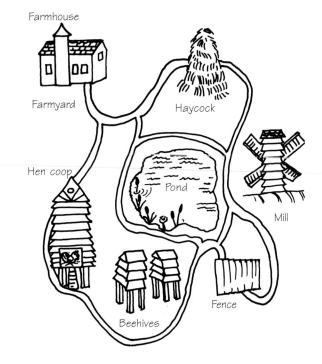

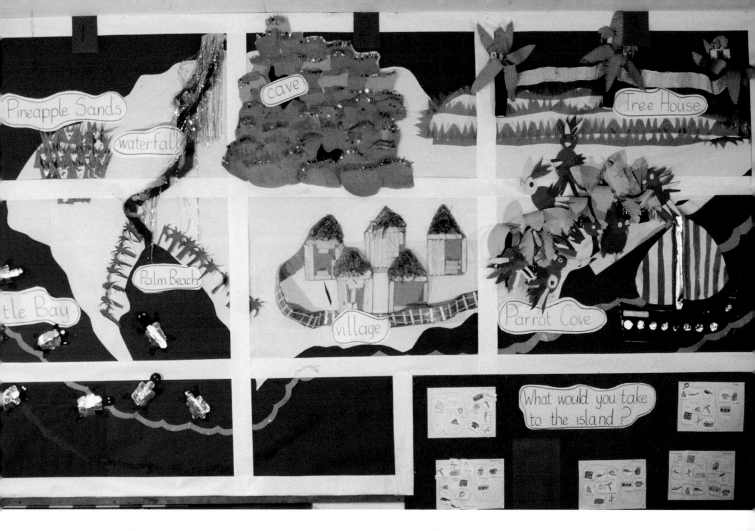

3 **An imaginary island**

Make a large wall map of an imaginary island (see above) either to go with a published story or as a creative exercise. Include details such as houses and boats as well as hills, rivers, woods and other natural features. Give each place a name that reflects its character and draw a compass indicating north. Older children could research an area of the world in which their island lies and choose realistic animals, occupations and land use for authenticity.

4 **Grid references**

Add grid squares to any picture map. It is probably best to use the alpha-numeric system (ABC, 123, etc.) for early years classes. Children make a quiz for their friends in which they give the references of particular items or vice versa. You could also ask each child to write a detailed description of one of the squares. Can the rest of the class identify the square in question?

5 **Co-ordinate games**

There are quite a number of computer games based on grid references that are designed to develop co-ordinate skills. 'Pirate Gold', one of the sub-programs on *Maths with a Story 2* (ATMS), is particularly recommended as it provides the player with feedback. Alternatively you could introduce the children to the game of 'battleships', which only needs a ruler, paper and a pencil.

6 **Grid reference routes**

Draw a grid with reference numbers on the lines rather than on the spaces. Mark a starting and a finishing point, add pictures of obstacles and cover with a transparent seal. Children use a Chinagraph pencil to trace a route through the obstacles, listing the grid references as they go. They then rub out the Chinagraph route and ask another child to follow their directions.

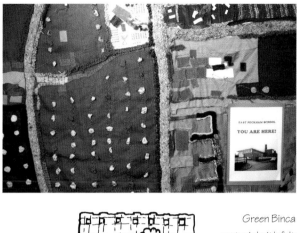

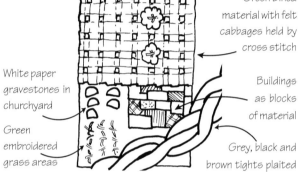

Green Binca material with felt cabbages held by cross stitch

White paper gravestones in churchyard

Green embroidered grass areas

Buildings as blocks of material

Grey, black and brown tights plaited

Local area maps

1 Village collage

The map above was made from fabric. Children knitted the roads in grey wool, used small pieces of cotton for the orchards and embroidered the gardens of houses. The background is green hessian with a frame made of old tights. The pattern of roads, fields and houses was based on the large-scale (1:1,250) Ordnance Survey map of the area. The children also explored the area on foot, adding photographs and descriptions of the fields and buildings to the display.

2 Aerial photographs

Children enjoy looking at aerial photographs and spotting the things they know. Find an aerial view of your local area and get the children to make a list of 15 or 20 key features. You can also ask them to trace routes, discuss when the picture was taken and record any changes they notice.

3 Street model

The model on page 61 was built on top of an enlarged map of the school locality. Each building was made from folded card. Crumpled paper and green scourers were used for hedges. The nets of building shapes provided a link with maths.

4 Maps and photographs

Compare a local aerial photograph with a map of the same area. One group can record 'what we see on the map but not on the photograph'. The second group can record 'what we see on the photograph but not on the map'. After the activity the two groups compare their findings.

5 Colour coding

Colour code local maps to show residential, industrial and shopping areas. Significant landmarks or buildings can be starred and labelled.

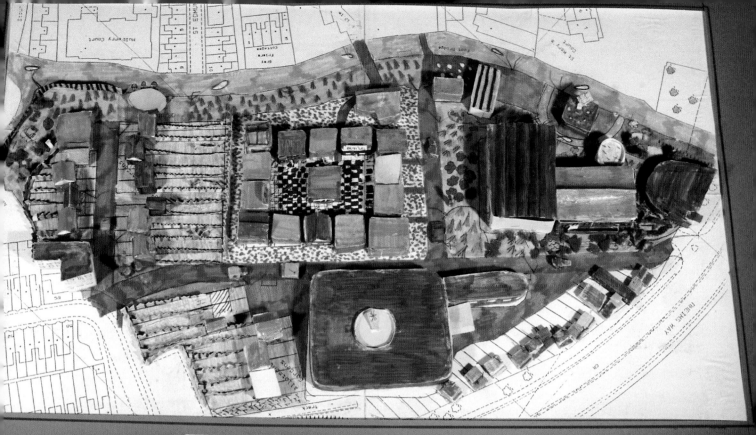

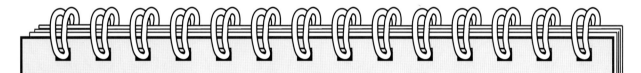

Our local area

Teaching plan

Enquiry question	Learning objective	Pupil activities
What do things look like from above?	Recognise plan views.	• Drawing around objects • Making model scenes
What is the difference between a picture and a map?	Maps use symbols, labels, grids and keys and are usually drawn in plan.	• Making a map of a scene • Making fabric maps and models
What do maps show?	Maps show the features of real or imaginary places.	• Making maps of the local area • Making imaginary maps

Around the world

Journeys

1 World journey

Are there any parents or visitors at your school who are going abroad? Equip a toy animal with a rucksack and send it on a world journey. You need to prepare a letter asking the traveller to take the toy to a suitable destination. The traveller should then pass the toy and the letter on to another person and send a postcard to the children giving an account of the place he or she is visiting. Stipulate in the letter that you would like the toy sent back to school at the end of a given period.

2 Passports

Bring a passport into school to show the class and discuss how it is used. Now get the children to make passports of their own, giving their address and place of birth. The children could add imaginary stamps to show the places they would like to visit.

3 Sammy's world journey

The display below shows the journey made by a toy bear called Sammy. The children arranged the postcards they received around a map and found out about the places he visited. Each destination provided the focus for some detailed research into its temperature, products, country flag, language and customs.

Focus

- Global awareness
- Using atlases and globes
- Journeys
- Customs and traditions

Word bank

barrier
country
globe
journey
passport
route

4 Travel agents

Tell the children that they are setting up a travel agent business and will need to prepare a holiday brochure. Get them to list the attractions of the different places they have selected. You could divide the children into groups and get them to present their schemes to another class.

Different places

1 Ring around the world

The picture above formed part of a class assembly. The children brought dolls and figures from different countries to school, made a ring around a globe and said a few words about what they had learnt. For further details, see *The Infant Assembly Book* by Doreen Vause (Macdonald 1985).

2 Whole-school displays

A series of wall displays around a school hall can depict customs and climate in other countries and perhaps reflect the origins of some families or links in your school. The underlying theme is that people have the same needs all over the world even if they live their lives differently.

3 Table displays

On a display table make a circle of paper plates, with each plate containing produce from a different country. Stand a globe in the centre and fix ribbons from countries to produce. Repeat the idea with flags or plants.

4 Globe game

Throw an inflated plastic globe to one of the children in the class. Now select a letter of the alphabet, either by drawing pieces of paper from a hat or by using a spinner. Can the child find a country or city on the globe that begins with that letter? When the child has answered successfully, he or she throws the globe to someone else.

Around the world

5 Postcard display

Build up a collection of postcards featuring scenes from around the world such as beaches, mountains, volcanoes and famous buildings. Get the children to write labels naming the place and country shown on each postcard and arrange the work around a world map.

The world has enough for everyone's need but not for everyone's greed.

6 Souvenirs

Build up a collection of souvenirs from different countries. Use the collection for observation and enquiry work. Get the children to select one of the souvenirs and study it, using the headings 'What I know', 'What I can guess' and 'What I want to know'.

7 Sharing the world

Divide the children into pairs and ask each pair to find out about an endangered animal. You can structure their research by using questions such as: What does it eat? Where does it live? Why is it in danger? What can be done to protect it? Put up a world map so that the children can point to the place where their animal lives when they report back to the rest of the class. You could also present the work as a class assembly, using a banner with these words from Gandhi: "The world has enough for everyone's need but not for everyone's greed".

I guess that it wasn't a good or bad luck charm.

I know this is made of wood

If it is based on a bird I would like to know what bird it is based on.

It tells me that the South-East Asian people probably liked art

What I know   What I guess

What I want to know

Around the world

Christmas

1 Where does Father Christmas come from?
Discuss with the children where Father Christmas or Santa Claus lives. Can they find Lapland on a map? To show his journey to your area, make a picture map featuring the seas, rivers, mountains and other obstacles he has to cross.

2 Father Christmas's snowmobile
Design a snowmobile for Father Christmas that will be suitable for travel on snow and ice, through blizzards and over rooftops. It must have room for Christmas parcels and space for emergency gear in case the route is blocked by snowdrifts.

3 Christmas cards
Trace the route of a Christmas card from another country to your school. What places, sights, languages and boundaries would it encounter?

4 Christmas weather
Use a globe or a world map to point out which places are hot and which places are cold at Christmas. Colour the places red or blue and make a key.

5 Christmas in the Ukraine
The display below shows how people celebrate Christmas in the Ukraine. Each child made a cut-out of a person holding 'shaking paper tassels' made by curling paper around a pencil. The border was decorated with stars, which were made from circles of shiny silver paper folded three times into a wedge and then cut with scissors to remove pieces on the circumference.

6 Christmas in New Zealand

How do children spend Christmas Day in New Zealand? Make a life-size display of a beach scene like the one above by drawing around a child who is lying on a sheet of paper. Then cut out two silhouettes, crumple up pieces of newspaper to pad out the model, staple the outlines together and paint or wax crayon the skin. Dress the model with suitable clothes for a picnic.

7 St Nicholas's Day

On 5 December people in the Netherlands celebrate St Nicholas's Day. Tradition has it that Black Peter, the saint's helper, calls on each home and throws in sweets for the children. Add sweets to your display for extra interest! Or try another Dutch custom. Each child leaves a shoe in the classroom for 5 December with a note inside saying what he or she would like for Christmas. The next day the note should have been replaced by a sweet left by Black Peter.

Teaching plan

Enquiry question	Learning objective	Pupil activities
How do places differ around the world?	Weather, landscape, language and customs vary from place to place.	• Using maps and globes • Research and enquiry skills
In what ways are places similar?	All people have festivals and celebrate their lives.	• Christmas in different places

A place at the seaside

Focus

- Seashore environment
- Pollution
- Place studies

Word bank

beach
habitat
holidays
jobs
pollution
rock pool
tide
zone

1 Where is Wembury?

Wembury is a seaside village on the south-west coast of England not far from Plymouth. The display above shows some of the main buildings by the sea such as the church, stables, cafe and toilets. The drawings around the edge show holiday activities and are taken from the Infant Geography Resource Bank (Stanley Thornes 1994).

2 Why visit Wembury?

Children can use the display to: (a) plan days at the beach; (b) list the things they would take to Wembury on holiday; (c) design and write a postcard; and (d) match leisure activities to locations or buildings. They can also locate Wembury on a map and work out the distance to their own town/city and to major cities in the UK where visitors might come from.

3 Jobs in Wembury

Get the children to make a portrait gallery showing where people in Wembury work and the jobs they do.

4 Beach pastimes

Create some large shell templates. Ask the children to trace these shapes to make frames in which they can draw and write about the things they could see and do at the beach. Make a border for the display from shell shapes coloured with wax crayons.

5 Beach transect

There are a number of zones or habitats on the beach from the low-water mark upwards. Children can create a frieze that shows these different areas, adding shells, driftwood, egg cases, seaweed and other things they have collected on a visit.

6 The seashore code

Making posters that show the seashore equivalent of the country code will encourage young people to care for our coastal environment. Include a reminder to return creatures to the sea after looking at them.

7 Rock pool role-play

Some children join hands to form a rocky pool while others become the creatures inside. Get the class to act out what happens as the tide comes in and out. Extend the activity by getting the children to show the effect of storms on cliffs.

8 Rock pool paintings

Create rock pool paintings by blowing bubbles in water mixed with blue paint. Then lower a sheet of paper carefully on to the bubbles until they burst. Spare bubble prints make an attractive border for a seashore wall display.

9 Beach rubbish

Make a collection of the rubbish and debris that are often washed up on to the beach at high tide. Get the children to sort the collection into natural and manufactured items. Can they estimate how long things take to rot in the sea? Extend the work with a story link. *One World* by Michael Foreman (Andersen 1990) is relevant.

10 The rubbish monster

Children at Wembury cleaned up the beach. With help from the Devon Wildlife Trust warden, they then made a monster to show the public the things that spoil the beach. Here is an idea for any environment spoilt by rubbish.

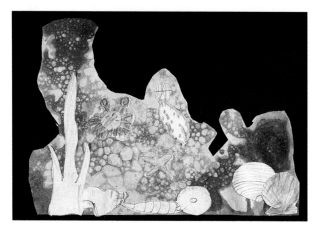

Teaching plan

Enquiry question	Learning objective	Pupil activities
Why do people go to the seaside for their holidays?	People enjoy swimming, playing in the water and exploring the seashore.	• Beach pastimes • Case study of Wembury
What is the seashore like?	There are cliffs and beaches and many different seashore creatures.	• Rock pool paintings and role-play • Beach transects
Why do we need to care for the seashore?	Litter and pollution affect the wildlife.	• Rubbish surveys/pollution experiments

A place in France

1 Flags

Working out from the flagpole, the French flag is blue, white and red. Children can decorate their flags with pictures of famous French buildings and traditional French produce. This helps to develop their images of France.

2 Using photographs

Make a display of photographs of France using either pictures cut out from tourist brochures or photographs you have taken yourself when visiting France. Get the children to print out labels for each photograph from a computer. They could also add enquiry questions to investigate in topic work.

3 *En ville*

Design symbols for different French buildings and shops such as a bakery, a café and a pharmacy. Children can create a street (la rue) or a town square (la place), cutting and pasting their symbols to create imaginary maps.

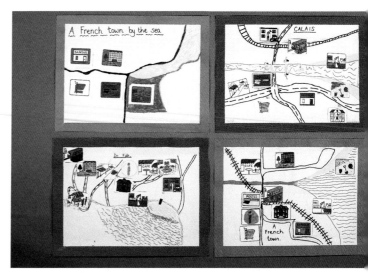

4 Getting there

Draw a large outline map of the Channel. Add pictures around the edge showing all the ways of crossing it - even by swimming! The work can be differentiated into the following tasks: (a) drawing and cutting out pictures; (b) labelling each means of transport; (c) choosing one route and explaining its advantages and disadvantages; and (d) finding out about the time and price of each journey.

5 Shopping

Create a French shop in your home corner. *La Boulangerie* can be stocked with playdough baguettes, croissants and gateaux - all words children may be familiar with. Compare the products with those in a British bakery. (Opening times in France are usually 8 a.m. to 12 noon and 2 p.m. to 6 p.m. or even later.)

Teaching packs

Montreuil (Geographical Association)
European Locality Pack: Wasquehal near Lille
(Ginn)

Focus

- Food and shopping
- Landscapes
- Maps and symbols
- European awareness

Word bank

customs
ferry
landscape
market
square
symbol

6 Francs

Cardboard coins showing French francs and centimes make a useful addition to the bakery. Children can copy them on to a homemade bingo card with nine squares. A game of coin bingo helps number recognition in English in the early years, and in French later on. French children shout 'loto' when their card is full.

7 A French breakfast

Turn your classroom into a French café and invite some mums, governors or just the class for breakfast. You could decorate the walls with French paintings and play some French music in the background. Cover the tables with blue, white and red frieze paper and serve orange juice, hot chocolate, baguettes or croissants on napkins (no plates).

8 *Un plan de la ville*

Decorate a street map of a French town with symbols for different features.

9 French landscapes

Link with art by considering the landscape paintings of some famous French artists. A class used the technique of painting in dots to produce their landscapes in the display below. Start a gallery of paintings in the style of Seurat or Monet.

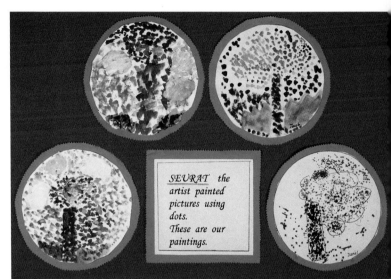

SEURAT the artist painted pictures using dots. These are our paintings.

10 Stories

Red Riding Hood and *Sleeping Beauty* were both written by the French author Perrault. The sleeping beauty's castle is at Ussé in the Loire Valley. Joan of Arc met the Dauphin at Chinon, won a great battle against the English at Orléans and was put to death at Rouen. Children may like to write a story set in a French castle, using French names, food and buildings.

Teaching plan

Enquiry question	Learning objective	Pupil activities
What is special about France?	The French have their own language, food and customs.	• Stories and paintings • Food tasting • French vocabulary
What are traditional French towns like?	French towns have markets, cafés and small shops.	• Making maps and symbols

A place in Egypt

Focus
- Weather
- River Nile
- Using artefacts

Word bank
camel
cotton
dam
desert
galabaih
Nile
spice
temperature
temple

3 The spice market
Set up a table display with small piles of herbs and spices to emulate a stall in Aswan market. Children squeeze and smell the different spices and role-play a trader encouraging passers-by to make a purchase.

4 *Karcade*
Egyptian farmers grow fields of hibiscus to make this popular drink. To make your own *karcade*, use dried hibiscus flowers from a health food shop. One handful of flowers (or one tablespoon of powdered flowers) boiled in one litre of water, then strained, makes a warm tea or an iced cordial. Add sugar to taste. Get the children to make a decorated bar chart showing who likes or dislikes the drink.

1 Making a parcel
Make up a parcel containing a range of interesting items from Egypt. The parcel can be unwrapped gradually as the topic unfolds, making a display of items on a table. Visit a health food store, the Egyptian tourist office or the British Museum shop to obtain the things you need. Alternatively give a shopping list (and a roll of film) to someone who is going to Egypt.

2 The parcel
The parcel above contains items either bought by tourists in Egypt or obtained in the UK:
spices and herbs - turmeric, coriander, saffron, hibiscus, indigo;
produce - limes, potatoes, dates;
artefacts - Nile map, local newspaper, cotton clothes, postcards, photographs, coins, soapstone ornaments, papyrus items.

5 A story to read
The Day of Ahmed's Secret by Florence Parry Heide (Gollancz 1991) evokes the atmosphere of Cairo and has good illustrations for research use. Give the children some activity cards to use with the book. Questions could include: How do people move heavy goods around? What are the different things sold in the market?

Teaching packs
Egypt: Luxor (Folens)
The Thread of the Nile (Birmingham Development Education Centre)
Cairo: Four Children and their City (Oxfam)

6 Hot weather

Collect temperature recordings for Cairo or Luxor from a daily newspaper. Use a data handling program to make a bar chart of the readings. Get the children to write about their findings, perhaps making comparisons with their own area.

7 Egyptian clothes

Talk with the children about the need for cool, flowing clothes in extremely hot climates. You can make an Egyptian *galabaih* quite simply from a sheet (see below). After wearing one, children will be better able to understand the advantages of loose garments.

8 River Nile

Make a large wall map of the River Nile. Young children can make paintings to go round the edge. Older children can use travel guides and atlases to add details about the temples, crops, cities and country boundaries.

9 Life in the desert

The River Nile brings life to the desert. Use a large tray filled with sand and some fast-growing seeds such as cress to demonstrate this to the class. First sprinkle the sand with the seeds. Then carefully water it each day in a thin line marked by a length of string. Watch what happens and keep a record of plant growth.

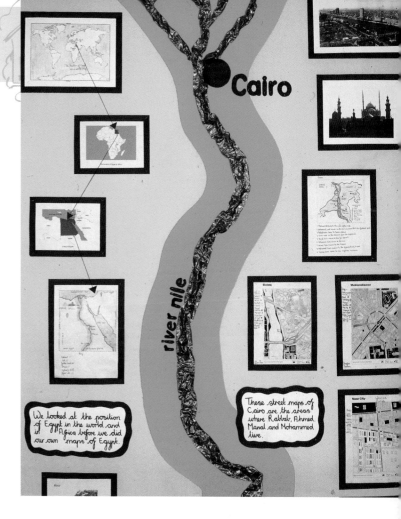

Pattern for a galabaih

Wrist to wrist

Cut two of these shapes

Underarm to ankle   Underarm to wrist

Cut slit, then sew shapes together

Teaching plan

Enquiry question	Learning objective	Pupil activities
What clues tell us about a distant place?	Everyday items provide information about people's lives.	• Unwrapping a parcel • Display table • Making karcade
How does the weather affect life in Egypt?	Egyptians wear clothes and grow crops that are suitable for a hot place.	• Weather statistics • Cotton clothes and spice market
How is the River Nile important to Egypt?	People, plants and animals depend on water from the Nile.	• Growing experiments • Maps and reports

A place in Kenya

Focus

- Tourism
- Endangered species

Word bank

brochure
coast
mountain
produce
safari park
souvenir
tourist

1 Display table

Here are some ideas for a Kenya display table like the one above:

local produce - dwarf beans, tea, coffee, pineapples, tropical fruit juices;

craft items - pottery, cloth, necklaces, baskets, musical instruments;

everyday objects - stamps, coins, cassette tapes, newspapers, school books.

2 Working from clues

The children each choose one of the items from the display table. They then complete a report sheet by dividing their page into four sections: (a) detailed drawing; (b) written description; (c) questions about the object; and (d) answers to the questions.

3 Mount Kenya model

Build a model of Mount Kenya. Start by cutting off the front of a cardboard box. Then pile up crumpled newspaper, egg boxes or chicken wire on the base to make a mountain shape. Finally cover with layers of newspaper and paint. Show how the vegetation changes at different levels on the mountain - snow at the top, then alpine plants, then evergreen trees, then deciduous trees and finally rainforest.

Model of Mount Kenya

Box with front removed

4 Tourist brochures

Divide the class into groups. Each group produces a leaflet to attract tourists. Suitable enquiry questions include: Where is Kenya? How long does it take to get there? What wild animals live in the safari parks? How does the weather vary through the year? What is the coast like? What places can you visit in Kenya?

5 Suitcase

Pack a suitcase for a holiday in Kenya. Ask the children to consider the weather, prepare for a safari visit and take a medical kit. This activity could lead to a class display, individual labelled pictures or a computer printout.

6 Safari parks

Children cut out animals found in safari parks from templates or photocopied sheets. Inside each animal shape they record its colour, food, life cycle and other interesting facts. Display the work as a frieze on a safari park landscape.

7 Kenya map

Make a large outline map of Kenya for a wall display. Get the children to find out about the weather, landscape and other factors that affect tourism.

8 Jobs in tourism

Get each child to take on the role of one of the people working in the Kenyan tourist industry. Jobs include hotel staff, minibus drivers, safari park wardens, souvenir sellers and tribal dancers. Each child should then write a job advertisement - describing what he or she does - to go in the *Nairobi Times*.

9 Tourist problems

Two groups of children prepare an illustrated speech on the issue of tourism in safari parks. One group has to argue for a growth in tourism, the other for restrictions.

Teaching packs

Kaptalamwa (Geographical Association); *Nairobi* (Action Aid); *Kapsokwony* (Action Aid); *Kenya* (BBC supports 'Zig Zag' TV programme); *Feeling Good about Faraway Friends* (Leeds Development Education Centre)

Teaching plan

Enquiry question	Learning objective	Pupil activities
Where is Kenya?	Kenya is a country in Africa.	• Using an atlas or globe
How is Kenya different from the UK?	Kenya has mountains, plains, safari parks and tropical beaches.	• Research for mapmaking • Tourist advertisements • Packing a suitcase
Why do tourists go to Kenya?	Tourists go to see the wild animals and enjoy the beaches.	• Jobs in tourism • Tourist problems

A place in India

1 Chembakolli village

The display below shows a children's collage of a village in southern India. Maps and photographs in the *Chembakolli* locality pack (Action Aid) provided the background information together with pictures in story books.

Focus

- Weather
- Animals
- Village life
- Change
- Using photo packs

Word bank

elephant
environment
monsoon
pump
tiger
water supply
wildlife

3 Monsoon

In India people depend on the monsoon to bring rain for crops. Make a dial to show the different seasons and add symbols and pictures for illustration. The children could collect temperature statistics for specific Indian cities from the newspaper. They could also make a comparable dial showing English weather.

2 Using photographs

You can turn the photographs from the *Chembakolli* pack into a reference book. Get the children to sort the photographs into sets such as 'weather', 'landscape' and 'jobs' and ask them to write their own captions. This is one way of making material intended for juniors suitable for use with infants.

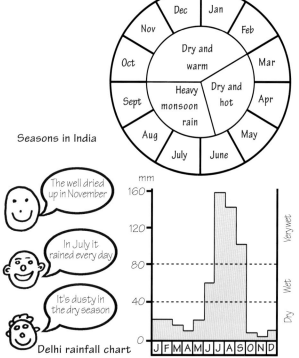

Seasons in India

The well dried up in November

In July it rained every day

It's dusty in the dry season

Delhi rainfall chart

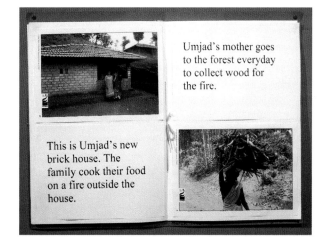

Umjad's mother goes to the forest everyday to collect wood for the fire.

This is Umjad's new brick house. The family cook their food on a fire outside the house.

4 Water supply

Some people in India have to collect all their water from a pump or well. Fill a bucket or can with water and get the children to carry it around the edge of the playground. How many litres did they carry and what was the weight of the water? How many journeys would they have to make to get enough water for a bath?

5 Indian food

Visit a street market or bring into school some Indian produce such as coconuts, mangoes, bananas, sweet potatoes, stem ginger, chillies, peppers and spices. Label the items and look in cookery books to find out how each one is used.

6 Making tea

Make a display of different Indian teas in small pots with labels inviting the children to squeeze and smell. Find out how tea is produced, perhaps by contacting a tea importer or the Commonwealth Institute. Round off the work by making a pot of tea for a tasting session.

7 Fact file

Using an atlas and reference books, make a fact file about India. The file could name the highest mountain, the longest river, the main cities and so on. Get the children to devise their own questions and see if they can find the answers.

Teaching packs

Chembakolli (Action Aid); *Bangalore: Indian City Life* (Action Aid); *Ladakh Photopack* (Geographical Association); *A Tale of Two Cities: Calcutta and London* (Birmingham Development Education Centre)

8 Threatened wildlife

In the past elephants were used as working animals in India. Now they are threatened with extinction, along with tigers and other wildlife, as forests are felled for timber. Find out what is happening from the Worldwide Fund for Nature (WWF) and reference books, or read *The People Who Hugged the Trees* by Deborah Lee Rose (Rinehart 1991) to the children.

9 Animal art

The elephant below was made by glueing pieces of newspaper on to an outline shape. A tiger could be made by using orange paper from magazines or wrappers from Crunchie bars.

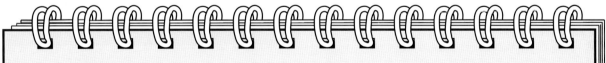

Teaching plan

Enquiry question	Learning objective	Pupil activities
What is India like?	India is famous for its food, products, customs and monsoon.	• Fact file • Indian food and tea • Weather studies
How do people live in Indian villages?	Villagers grow their own food, collect water from a well and live in scattered houses.	• Photo pack • Maps, plans and collage pictures • Comparison with cities
How is the environment changing?	Cities are growing larger. Wildlife is threatened.	• Fact file and place studies

A place in the rainforest

Focus

- Rainforest habitats
- Environmental issues

Word bank

environment
jungle
rainforest
reserve
species
zoo

1 Jungle corner

The reading corner on the right has been turned into a jungle. A net strung across the ceiling represents the canopy of trees, while creepers made from green crêpe paper hang down. The walls are decorated with poems about animals. There are messages inviting the children to look at the book display. One message is written on a snake shape and encourages children to 'curl up with a book'.

2 Rainforests

Divide the children into groups and ask each group to conduct its own research into the rainforests. Use headings such as: 'A fascinating creature', 'An unusual plant', 'An interesting fact', 'An environmental concern' and 'A jungle home' to focus the children's attention. Get each group to add its work to a display around a map of the world's rainforests.

Teaching plan

Enquiry question	Learning objective	Pupil activities
Why are the rainforests so important?	Many different plants and creatures live in the rainforests.	• Research • Rainforest stories • Garden visit
How can the rainforests be saved?	Rainforests need to be used sustainably.	• Role-play and discussions • Making posters

My jungle book

3 My jungle book

Young children can create their own books with attractive cover designs. Each inside page deals with a different plant or animal. A large feather duster was the basis for the parrot model above. Elephant silhouettes make an effective border for written work. A coiled snake falls from an opened page.

4 Zoo animals

Zoos represent one way of protecting endangered animals. Story books can stimulate discussion on the ethics of keeping animals in zoos. The children can then make models and masks of the animals with poems displayed on the models to blend in with the shape or patterns on the body.

5 Jungle plants

Visit a botanical garden with a glasshouse to see plants from the rainforests. Alternatively make a display of indoor plants that come from the jungle such as African violets, orchids, Swiss cheese plants and Venus fly-traps. Draw the plants and add labels to show how they have adapted to the weather and light conditions.

6 Living in the rainforest

Use reference books to help make 'profiles' of the people who live in the rainforest. Each profile should include a picture of a person and details of his or her home, food and daily life. Stories such as *Antonio's Rainforest* by Anna Lewington (Wayland 1992) can help provide additional information.

7 Forest clearance

Create a role-play on the problems of deforestation. Suitable characters to include are a timber merchant, a builder who needs wood for homes, a cattle rancher wanting more open land, and a government official in charge of roads and railways. For every view, an opposing conservationist makes an objection. Translate this into a 'for and against' display poster with opposing speech bubbles.

Teaching packs

Focus on Castries, St Lucia (Geographical Association)
Go Bananas! (Oxfam)

Studying distant places

Children need to learn about distant places to develop a broad and balanced understanding of the world. The ideas in the 'Places' section of this book (pages 68-79) can be adapted to fit whichever locality you choose to study. The plan below provides a checklist of key questions to help you devise your own scheme of work.

India — Using a photo pack, Weather, Products

France — Using photographs, Language, Buildings

Egypt — Weather, Parcels, Rivers

Seaside — Environmental concerns, Jobs, Tourism

Kenya — Tourism, Animals, Artefacts

Rainforest — Animals, Conservation, Plants

Enquiry question	Learning outcome	Pupil activities
What is the place like?	Places have distinctive landscape features. Each place has its own settlement and land use pattern.	• Use photographs, maps and atlases to study the character of a place • Use artefacts as a source of evidence
Who lives in the place and what are their lives like?	People live in a variety of homes and have different daily diets and timetables. Some jobs depend on local resources.	• Role-play of people in their jobs • Farming in different places • Effect of weather on houses
How is the place linked to other places?	Roads, railways and other routes link places together.	• Use world maps to locate places and routes that tourists take • Use locality study packs
How is the place similar to or different from where I live?	People meet their needs in different ways in different environments.	• Compare homes, schools, clothes, food and language
How is the place changing?	Places change all the time. Some changes are slow, others are dramatic.	• Study of changes brought about by natural forces, tourism and habitat destruction